Gree...
Adventure

Greenlands Adventure

Cathie Bartlam

Scripture Union
130 City Road, London EC1V 2NJ.

By the same author:

Maggie Magpie – (*6–8s*)
Operation Sandy – *Tiger Book*
Tricky Business – *Tiger Book*
Go for Gold – *Leopard Book*
Stranded! – *Leopard Book*

© Cathie Bartlam 1992
First published 1992

ISBN 0 86201 741 6

Phototypeset by Intype, London
Printed and bound in Great Britain by Cox & Wyman Ltd, Reading

1

'When will it be here, Miss?' Sal asked for the fourth time. 'It's nearly half past. You said half past.'

Miss Winter was looking flustered. 'Soon,' she said automatically, her eyes scanning the assortment of children, parents, bags and even a couple of dogs, all milling around in the playground.

4N were going to Greenlands. Four whole days, three nights at the adventure camp deep in the heart of the country. Every year the top juniors went to Greenlands. It was a tradition, a treat, something wonderful to look forward to. Well it was for Sal and her gang. Miss Winter, however, did not look so enthusiastic.

'Billy, get your dog off the sleeping bags! Vicki! *Three* suitcases?'

'I might get dirty,' said Vicki, as immaculate as ever in a new track suit.

'Will, if I have anything to do with it,' said Sal. 'You're first on my list to go in the lake.'

'You'll have to catch me then!' Vicki sprinted off, leaping over her luggage with surprisingly little effort for a large girl.

'What's up with her?' asked Narrinder, who was whirling her long dark plaits as usual. When she was excited, she spun them so fast that they became a blur. She was excited today.

'Aw, nothing,' replied Sal. 'I'll get her later.'

'You've not fell out again, have you?' Narrinder was anxious.

'Course not.' Sal was surprised her best friend could

think such a thing. The arch enemy of last term, the previously hated Vicki, was now firmly part of the gang. And one of the main rules was never to break friends.

A huge cheer erupted from the playground as the coach came into view. Thirty children rushed towards it, all at the same speed, tripping over each other in their haste to be first on the coach. Abandoned parents called out last minute instructions.

'Phone up when you get there!'

'Don't forget to change your underwear!'

'Marie! You've left your lunch here.'

Tom's mum insisted on kissing him in front of everyone. He was horrified and turned beetroot red, shamed and embarrassed.

'Right. Quiet!' bellowed Miss Winter. 'No one's going anywhere yet. We've a lot to do. The rest of the staff will get you organised. Mr Wilkins, Peter's dad, is in charge of the luggage. He will get you all sorted out.'

This proved to be a mammoth task. The kit list for camp had said to bring a few changes of old clothes. By the look of the holdalls, suitcases, plastic bin bags and carrier bags, most of the children had emptied the contents of their wardrobes into whatever container was available.

Mr Wilkins stuffed most of it into the coach boot, climbing into its dark cave-like interior, bent double like a gorilla. He took ages, stacking things neatly. Sal got impatient.

'Let's shut him in with it,' she urged Cowboy and Tag, also members of the gang. 'I'll scream if he takes much longer.'

'Thought the tricks were over,' said Cowboy.*

'I'm only joking, you pudding,' Sal said, pushing him playfully. 'Look, he's done.'

The boot was shut.

*See *Tricky Business*, the first story about Sal and friends.

'Now the sleeping bags.' Mr Wilkins stacked them carefully on the luggage racks. He piled those left over on the coach floor.

'Are we ready, Miss?' Sal asked, grasping Miss Winter's arm to get her attention. 'Can we go?'

'Soon,' came the reply that meant nothing. 'Right. 4N, make a straight line. Then, and only then, can you get on the bus.'

Sal, Vicki and Brian were first in the queue, mainly because they pushed past everyone else, ignoring their protests.

'We'll keep the back row,' Sal yelled. 'Narrinder, Tag, Cowboy, did you hear? The back row. Brill. I'm in the middle!'

That's what Sal thought.

'Right, 4N, about turn.' The class just stared open mouthed at Mr Wilkins. 'About turn! Do you lot understand? Turn round. That's right. The back is now the front. Got it?' He paused as the children worked out what he was doing. 'Right, Jayne and Tom, lead the way. Yes, you two. Pick your seats.'

Sal was furious. What a trick! Now she would get the worst seat. The back and front would be taken and she and the gang would end up with all the odd seats in the middle.

Sal was correct. Trampling over the mountain of sleeping bags, some escaping from their covers, like sausages poking out of sausage rolls, Sal found herself and Vicki right in the middle. As she sat down a sleeping bag unfurled itself from the luggage rack above her head and covered her thin wiry body. Sal fell over, landing on Brian's lap. Wolf-whistles echoed around the coach and Sal felt a real wally as she struggled to her feet.

Miss Winter took the register. 'Where's Rachel?'

'Gone to the loo.'

'And Peter? Mr Wilkins, where's your Peter?'

'Just nipped home, forgot our lunch.'

Miss Winter sighed but brightened visibly as a young man with wild curly hair, wearing a tatty pair of denim jeans and a jumper three sizes too big, poked his head around the door.

'Hi, everyone!'

'Ah, Da . . . Mr Rogers. Good to see you,' said Miss Winter.

'Bet it is!' yelled Cowboy.

'When are you two getting married?'

'Who'll do it? You can't marry yourself.'

David Rogers was the local curate who ran the church youth group. The class had got to know him last year when he had helped them with a project. He and Angela Winter had got engaged during the summer.

'Mr Rogers has come along to help keep an eye on you lot,' said Miss Winter, unsuccessfully trying not to blush. 'He knows how to deal with a rowdy bunch.'

Sal was glad that he was coming. Over the summer holidays she had gone along to the junior youth group and got to know David, as they called him there. He was good fun and had organised some great day trips for them. He was also helping Sal to understand a bit more about what it meant to be a Christian. Last term she had discovered that Jesus loved and understood her. He had helped her when she was in a mess and now she wanted to be one of his followers.

'Are we all ready then?' shouted Mr Rogers.

'Yes!' yelled the class.

'Not quite,' said Miss Winter. 'Be patient.'

'Why are we waiting? Why are we waiting?' bawled twenty-eight voices, with more volume than tune. Peter Wilkins appeared clutching a huge cool-box containing his own and his dad's lunch. There was enough to feed the entire bus.

Mrs Rowbottom finally turned up. She was the school secretary who had volunteered to help out. Sal was pleased that she was coming and not the head, Mrs

Preston. Mrs Preston was a force to be reckoned with. Mrs Rowbottom, although she thought she was stern, was in fact as soft as a brush, fussing around, but never getting mad if someone forgot their dinner money or needed help.

'Found Rachel,' she said, pushing a tearful girl in front of her. 'The loo door was stuck and she thought we had gone without her.' She paused. 'And we couldn't go without these.' She held aloft two cold clanking metal buckets.

'Not the sick buckets!'

'Aw, no, Miss.'

'I'm not sitting by Tom. He was sick last school trip,' said Jayne.

'No, I wasn't!'

'Yes, you was!'

'That was in the first year. I'm okay now,' protested Tom, as he was propelled to the front of the bus by his reluctant seat mate.

'Any one else likely to be sick?' asked Mrs Rowbottom.

For two seconds there was silence. The only silence there would be for the next four days.

'Right then, tell me if you feel queasy. Simon, how much chocolate have you eaten so far? Two bars? Well, give it a rest then.'

Mrs Rowbottom eased herself into the seat next to the unfortunate Tom, who gazed gloomily out of the window.

'We're ready!'

Parents waved, little brothers and sisters shouted goodbye. Marie's mum knocked on the window and told her she must take her asthma medicine. Other schoolchildren, trapped in their classrooms, pressed envious faces up to their windows and wished they were escaping from school.

Sal's mum had left ages ago to take Lizzie, her baby sister and the Littlies she minded, off to playgroup. Sal was too happy even to notice her mum had gone.

The coach door swung shut. Nothing happened.

'The driver! Where's the driver?'

Mrs Rowbottom was sent to find him. He had slipped outside for a stroll around the playground. It had taken so long to get everyone organised that the cook had taken pity on him. He was found, drinking his second cup of tea, telling the dinner-ladies tall stories about "coaches I have driven".

The driver pottered across to the bus, looking like a chubby penguin in his dark uniform. Mrs Rowbottom tried to hurry him along.

'Makes a good cuppa, your cook,' was his only comment as he got into his seat.

'I think we are ready,' said Miss Winter, and the coach slowly and majestically launched itself off down the narrow street, which was bordered by stone terraced houses.

It was a gorgeous September morning. Even the weather seemed to realise that today was a very special day. Sunlight patterned into the coach, the orange skylights giving everything a golden glow.

Sal's face was bathed in the yellow rays which showed up her freckles. There were so many of them that in places they had merged and it was impossible to tell where one ended and another began. Her gingery hair had grown during the holidays. Mum had tortured it into a French plait. It was a waste of time. Most of it had escaped and just a pointed tuft trapped by a green bobble stuck out at the back. They were all singing the 'one man went to mow' songs that went on and on. No-one could agree on the words so they made up their own version.

'One school went to Greenlands, went to Greenlands to camp,

One school and the teacher, secretary, curate and Peter Wilkins' dad,

Went away to Greenlands.'

More and more verses were added to include all the stuff they had brought with them, not forgetting the sick buckets.

Sal gazed out of the smeared window, wiping it with her sleeve. Even the town looked good today. The grey stone buildings appeared lighter. Here and there window boxes displayed the reds and blues of the last of the summer bedding plants. The usually dull roads looked like silver ribbons leading them to a new world. The derelict steelworks, its piles of rubble half hidden by a tall tottering wall, seemed like something from another planet.

In the middle of the old steelworks sprawled a giant bright green spider made of curved metal and glass. It was surrounded by huge hoardings.

'Look, Vicki,' said Sal. 'What's that?'

'It's where they're building the new shopping complex.' Vicki always read the newspapers. 'They've nicknamed it "The Arachnid".'

'The what?'

'Means spider.'

'Well, why don't they call it that, then?'

Vicki ignored her question. 'Do you know, Sal, thousands of men lost their jobs when it closed. The steelworks. Mum told me when we moved here last year.'

'Don't need to tell me that,' said Sal. 'My dad was one of them. He was lucky though. Got the lorry driving job. My Uncle Bill had to move miles away to get work. Lots of the older men never got anything.'

Sal did not want to talk about it. It made her feel sad. She had heard so many stories about the steelworks and now it was dead, and, some said, the town was dying with it. Today was a time for happy thoughts.

They were driving through the country now. Winding roads, little villages, fields with stone walls, clumps of woods, as if someone had just put them there. Miss

Winter had given them all a photocopied map to follow.

'We're on grid 5B,' she called, 'going south. That's down the page for you at the back. Try to spot the different landmarks.'

Sal had lost her map somewhere. Sharing Vicki's uncreased piece of paper, neatly fastened to a clip-board, she saw that there were miles to go. Rivers, bridges, stomach churning bends in the roads and a hold-up where some crazy Council had decided to dig up the road in the middle of nowhere.

One bend proved to be too much for Simon. 'Miss,' he gasped. 'I'm going to be . . .' and he was. Sick all over himself.

'Told you I was all right,' protested Tom, as the coach stopped. Simon was stripped to his boxer shorts, which were patterned with red elephants. Then he was washed down with disinfectant, wrapped in the nearest sleeping bag and made to sit at the front.

'Hey, that's my sleeping bag,' called Cowboy. 'I'm not using it now he's puked on it!'

'It's okay,' Mrs Rowbottom said. 'Swop or something. Anyway we're nearly there. Driver, carry on!'

Ten minutes later the coach slowed down. Sal looked out of her window. Miles of countryside. Nothing else. She stood up, trying to see out of the front. Trees, fields and more trees.

They headed straight for the trees and at the last minute the coach swerved onto a brown dirt track. A wooden carved sign hung motionless in the warm still air. It read 'Greenlands', and had an arrow beside it pointing to the deserted path.

The coach squeezed its way between the lines of trees, their tapering branches reaching out to tap the roof. It had gone darker, the sunlight blocked by the huge old beech and birch mixed with tall pines.

As soon as the tree tunnel ended, the coach stopped in a bit of a clearing. All Sal could see was a small hut.

Was this it?

'Here we are,' said Miss Winter. 'Just sit still for a few moments longer. Greenlands Adventure is about to begin.'

2

'Hello, everyone. You must be the terrors that we've been expecting from Auden Junior School.'

The coach door was being pushed open by a great big yellow and green striped bobble hat that had two pink ears sewn onto it. The top of the woollen hat flopped over into the eyes of its owner. His dark skin was shiny, sweat drops dripping from beneath the hat, and he beamed at the children, his massive frame blocking the doorway.

'I'm Kevin. You'll be seeing a lot of me over the next few days, so let's get going.'

'Going where?' called a voice from the back. 'There's nothing here.'

'That's what you think! The coach can't go further, so it's everyone out along with all your luggage. I'll open the tuck shop for a few minutes first.' And the hat unlocked the hut, pulled a long wooden cart out through the doors and flipped down a counter lid to display loads of pop and sweets.

A mass exodus of children emptied out of the coach. Kevin was buried under a forest of arms waving chocolate bars and money at him. At last he shut up shop. Meanwhile the driver, Mr Wilkins and Mr Rogers had unloaded the luggage.

'What do we do with this lot?' asked Mr Wilkins.

'The cart,' replied Kevin.

'The cart?'

'Yes, pile it on and then the horrors drag it up to the dorms. Path's too narrow for the coach.'

This sounded like fun to most of the children but Sal was too busy eating to get her stuff on the first load.

Kevin spied Simon, still wrapped in the sleeping bag. 'Not bedtime yet! What's the matter?'

'I was a bit sick.'

'A bit!' exclaimed Mrs Rowbottom. 'I'll have to find his clothes.'

Kevin picked up Simon and dropped him into the sleeping bag, as easily as if he were an insect in a matchbox. Tucking him under one arm, he placed him on top of the cart's luggage.

'Right, my lovelies. Heave ho! Simon's the chariot commander. Now, charge to the dorms.' And he helped pull the bouncing cart, with a much happier Simon rolling around on top, past the bend and out of sight.

'Come on,' said Sal. 'Let's follow. Did you see his hat? I've got to get one like it.'

'I haven't got my suitcases,' replied Vicki.

'They'll turn up.'

'I *must* have them.' Vicki was insistent.

'Suit yourself. I'm going to the dorms. Coming, Narrinder?'

Narrinder hesitated.

'Vicki will find our stuff.' Giving Vicki no choice in the matter, Sal ran off, dragging Narrinder with her.

The path led past a couple of fields to a courtyard surrounded by long low buildings.

'Let's try this,' said Sal, pushing open a door. 'It's no good, just a games room. Come on.'

'What's the rush?'

'Got to get a good bunk.'

'Well, why don't we go there?' Narrinder pointed to the sign that said Dormitories. That must be it.'

They barged through the door into a large square hallway where there were rows of low shelves. Opposite were two small rooms with just two beds in each.

'They're no good,' said Sal.

'Try here.' Narrinder pushed open the door to her right. A huge room stretched out as far as they could see. Metal bunk beds, with bare striped mattresses, occupied most of the space. Little sunlight filtered through the still closed curtains, which were horribly patterned in purple and red. The room smelt of wood and socks and adventure.

'We'll have these,' Sal ran to the end of the room and claimed a bunk in the corner. 'I'll go on top, you underneath. Vicki can be next to us.' And she climbed on her bunk, bouncing around on her bottom so her head did not hit the ceiling.

'Sally! Sally Musgrove!'

'Good grief. It's Miss Winter. Come on.' The two girls rejoined the rest of the class outside.

'Here's the sleeping plan,' began their teacher.

'But, Miss, we've chosen,' protested Sal.

'Can't we all choose?' asked Rachel.

'Go on, Miss.'

'Please.'

'All right.' Miss Winter gave up. As long as they all had a bed for the night, what did it matter? 'Girls on the right. Boys left. Staff in the middle. Twenty minutes, please, to sort yourselves out. Leave most of your things in their bags.'

Chaos reigned. No-one could find their own sleeping bag. They were nearly all blue. Vicki did not know what to do with her three suitcases so Sal stacked them one on top of another.

'Use up the first, then the next, don't fuss,' she said. Honestly, organising her gang got more difficult, not easier.

Sal dived into Narrinder's holdall.

'Thought your mum would send some of these.' And she helped herself to a handful of Indian sweets from Narrinder's parents' shop.

Rachel, who had stumbled in after the others, had got

the bunk under Vicki. Blinking through her thick glasses, she was slowly arranging a selection of cuddly toys on the end of her bed.

'What do you want those for?' said Sal, watching this process as if she could not believe her eyes.

'That's Horace and Jemima, Marvin and Mandy, Greta and Albert. I left the rest at home.'

'You softy!' Sal grabbed Albert, a plump furry hedgehog. 'Here, catch!' Albert sailed through the air landing somewhat unfortunately on Miss Winter's head as she entered the room.

'What the . . . Girls! I don't expect this . . .' She stopped. Sal had launched Greta, a squashed, nearly hairless, mouse-shaped object, before she had seen the teacher. Greta landed at Miss Winter's feet.

'I ought to have known. Where there is mischief, there is Sally Musgrove. Right, Sally?'

'I was only playing. Can I give them back to Rachel?'

'Yes. We'll have to make sure we tire you out, Sal. You won't have the energy left then for tricks.'

'No, Miss,' or should it have been 'Yes, Miss'? Sal was not bothered. Miss was all right really.

'Now girls, you can all go off and explore until lunch. The loud bell means come back to the dining room. That's next door by the games room. You've got half an hour or so. Disappear!' Miss Winter escaped to the safe haven of the dining area.

Sal, Narrinder and Vicki met up with Tag, Cowboy and Brian outside in the courtyard.

'Where shall we go first?' asked Tag, who as his nickname suggested, usually did what everyone else did.

'The woods.' Sal led the way round the back of the dormitory hut. There was a field scattered with trees and a few bushes.

'This ain't a wood,' said Cowboy. His mum had bought him a new selection of checked shirts over the summer. So now he either wore one much too short, or much too big. Today's effort was hanging over the ends of his well bitten fingernails.

''Tis then,' said Sal. 'Come on.'

They went through the field, round the back of the kitchens, crouching low so that no-one could see them. Then they came to the fields by the path.

'Horses!' Vicki ran towards them. 'Oh, they're lovely. Look Sal. Let's call them. Here, boy!'

The two horses lifted up their heads, pricked their ears forwards and ambled towards them.

'Come on, boy.' Vicki was really excited. She did not notice Sal backing away from the fence. 'Oh, you're a beaut.' Vicki sat astride the fence, stroking the great hairy head that gently butted at her stomach and slobbered down her new track suit.

'I wish I could ride them. Do you know I used to have lessons before we moved. I loved it. I could canter and jump and . . .'

Sal was not listening. While the others pulled up tufts of grass to feed the horses, she kept her distance. They were so big! Give her Rachel's stuffed pony any day.

'This is boring. Come on,' and off they went, leaving Vicki crooning over her new found friends.

They walked through the football field nearly all the way to the now closed tuck shop.

'Hey, what's this?' Brian was crouching down in front of a long wire enclosure with a sort of hutch at one end. 'Do you think it's rabbits?'

'Or guinea pigs,' suggested Tag. 'My cousin's got guinea pigs and gerbils and a frog and . . .'

'Shut up about your loopy cousin,' said Brian. 'I bet he hasn't got one of these.'

The five of them watched as two tiny brown furry creatures gambolled out of their den.

'Foxes,' whispered Narrinder. 'Baby foxes.'

'Cubs,' Brian informed them. 'Wonder what they're doing here?' He got a long thin twig and poked it through the wire. The cubs tumbled around it, rolling over and then leaping at it.

'Like puppies,' said Tag. 'My cousin's puppies . . .' but no-one was taking any notice, so he lapsed into silence.

Sal was spellbound by the cuddly animals. Much nicer than large stomping horses.

'Let's get one,' she said. 'Take it with us.'

'Can't. Don't be daft.'

But Sal had undone the wire gate and was in the enclosure. The cubs were tame and she quickly caught one and cradled it in her arms.

'I'll put it back soon. I promise. Just let me hold it for a bit.'

The rest of the gang knew there was no point arguing with Sal. They crossed the track, through another field and to a little bridge. A sluggish stream trickled over half submerged boulders that were covered in green spongy moss. Next to the bridge was a pipe that crossed the water.

'Follow the leader!' called Cowboy, and they chased over the bridge and back over the pipe, laughing and panting. Sal was the slowest, her hands occupied by the fox cub, and then the inevitable happened.

Wobbling on the pipe, she lost her balance and went straight into the water. Her trainers were soaked. Unable to use her arms to straighten herself up, she landed on her bottom in the couple of inches of surprisingly cold water.

At that moment a bell sounded, loud and penetrating.

'Lunch time. Sal, get up!' Narrinder tried to push Sal to her feet. Narrinder was useless as she did not want to get wet herself.

The bell rang again.

Sal sat there, shaking with laughter, clutching the precious cub to her chest, as the damp spread rapidly up from her feet and down from the backside of her jeans.

'Get up!' the others were impatient and set off. Sal jumped up and followed.

'The cub! What about putting him back?' asked Narrinder. There would be awful trouble and this was only the first day of the camp.

The bell rang yet again.

'After lunch. I'll take it back then.'

'But someone will see it. And your jeans.'

'They won't.' Sal put the cub up her jumper. 'When we get there, you walk in front of me, Nar, and Vicki, cover my rear. I'll get changed later.'

The cub settled down in his new woolly home, his claws scratching Sal through her T-shirt. Everyone else was in the dining room as the gang bunched through the doorway.

'I should have known who would be last,' said Miss Winter.

'Sorry Miss,' chorused the gang.

'Sit down. Now there's a mug of soup each, lots of sandwiches, a piece of cake and an apple.'

Mr Rogers said grace and they all tucked in.

'Brian, get the tomato out of this sandwich, will you?' asked Sal.

'Why?'

'Hate them, and I can't do it myself. Got to hold Foxy.'

'Perhaps he likes them,' suggested Brian.

'Shush.' The gang huddled closer together. Fortunately the rest of the class were too hungry to notice what was going on. However the staff were not.

David Rogers' eyes widened in amazement.

'Angela,' he said to Miss Winter. 'I don't know if I should tell you but that lad, the bright one with glasses . . .'

'Brian.'

'Well, he's stuffing bits of tomato up Sal's jumper.'

'David, stop having me on,' said his fiancee. 'Quite honestly if that's all she does on camp, I'll be relieved.'

'But it's moving.'

'What is?'

'The jumper.'

'Look, David, if she wants to put her entire lunch up her jumper, rather than inside her stomach, I'm not too bothered. Probably saving a bit for later.' Miss Winter dismissed the matter.

The noisy meal came to an end and the children stood.

'Clear the tables and wipe them,' called Miss Winter. 'We'll meet in ten minutes to sort out the activities.'

A ripple of laughter started in one corner, Sal's corner. It spread like a wave through the room.

'What's so funny?' asked Miss Winter.

'It's Sal.'

'She's been taken short.'

'Wet her pants!'

'Baby, baby, Sally, where's your little dummy?'

'Ah, shut up.' Sal turned, exposing her wet backside to full view. She was clutching her stomach. Her face was as red as the rejected tomato.

'Are you feeling all right?' Miss Winter enquired, and blinked rapidly. Surely she had not really seen a sliver of ham slide out of Sal's jumper onto the floor.

'Yes, Miss,' and Sal made a run for it. 'Find me some clothes,' she whispered to Vicki. 'Quick.'

Sal achieved the world record for running to the fox run, returning the cub, belting back to the dorm, getting changed and finding a spare pair of trainers. She lined up with the others, panting, unaware that her T-shirt was stained with tomato juice and covered in tiny brown hairs. Her jumper was slung casually round her neck. All her hair had escaped from its plait.

She grinned and winked at Vicki. This was a fantastic place. Wait until she had a go at some of the organised activities!

3

'Right everyone, pay attention!' Miss Winter waited as the noise and chattering subsided. 'In a few minutes we are going to hand you over to your instructors. Now, remember, what they say, you do. Understand?'

'Yes, Miss,' came the replies.

'Now all go and stand in your groups.' The class divided up into knots of children, about six in each group, all talking away.

'Hope we get canoeing.'

'I want the abseiling.'

'Marie, will you be my partner?'

'Do you think Mrs Rowbottom will join us?'

'Or Miss Winter?'

Tag, Cowboy, Brian, Vicki, Narrinder and Sal quickly made their own group. They had had a lot of fun together last year at school and were determined to enjoy every moment at Greenlands.

'Group One, Peter's, down to the lake with Kevin,' said Miss Winter.

'I wanted the lake,' whispered Sal.

'Group Two, Marie's, the assault course. Group Three, go with Mr Rogers to the river at the far end of the lake. Tom, you're group Four, follow me to the death slide . . .'

'Death slide?' Narrinder looked anxious. 'What on earth is that?'

'I shouldn't worry. We're not doing it,' replied Sal. 'Wonder what we are doing?'

'That just leaves Sal's group, number Five. Go down

to the field, the one opposite the horses, and you'll meet Bill,' Miss Winter informed them.

'And then what?'

'Archery.'

'Archery!' Sal exclaimed. 'But I don't want to do archery. I want to do canoeing or the death slide.'

'You'll get a turn at everything. Now run along.'

Sal stomped off, the gang following her.

'It's not that bad,' said Cowboy. 'We can pretend it's a film. A western. We can be Indians with bows and arrows.'

'Thought you were on the side of the cowboys, Cowboy,' interrupted Tag.

'Ha-ha, very funny,' Cowboy carried on. 'We can set up bases and come whooping over the hills . . .'

'There aren't any – hills I mean,' said Brian, practical as ever.

'And we can cover ourselves in warpaint,' Cowboy continued.

'And dance half naked around a totem pole.' Brian's sarcasm was wasted on Cowboy.

'Then capture the enemy and have a camp fire.'

'What enemy?' asked Tag.

'Well, he'll do,' and Cowboy pointed to the lone figure in the middle of the field.

The man was very tall, stood very straight and had grey stubbly hair in a short crew-cut.

'Not much point scalping him,' said Cowboy.

'Shut up.' Sal was fed up with them and their silly games.

The man moved towards them. He was wearing brown and green camouflage trousers and a green army style jumper with shoulder pads. Round his waist was a thick leather belt and clasped to it was a nine inch long dark green sheath.

'Look at his knife!' said Tag. 'My cousin's got one. Survival knife. In the Scouts.'

'Do you think he's in the wrong place?' asked Narrinder. 'He looks, well, a bit fierce.'

'Ah, troops!' boomed out a deep voice. 'Afternoon, chaps. You must be the advance party.' The children stared at him.

'I'm Bill, or sir, to you lot. Now stand to attention. Like so!' Bill clicked his heels together and stood like a concrete lamppost. The gang tried to copy him. Sal got a fit of the giggles and Vicki let out a yelp. She had clicked her heels together a bit too hard and was rubbing the inside of her ankle.

'You are the archery group?'

Nods all round.

'Well, let's make archers of you horrible lot,' bawled Bill, smiling at the same time. 'Done it before?' he paused. 'No? Raw recruits. What are we coming to?'

Bill gave them all a bow and arrow. 'Don't use them yet. See the targets?' They could hardly miss the row of coloured eyes at the far end of the field. 'Got to try to hit them.'

'What's the white stuff? You know, flapping behind the targets?' asked Brian.

'Sheets. All will be revealed. Now watch.' An arrow glided silently through the air, landing in the red circle on the target. Three more followed it, one hitting the gold.

'Looks dead easy,' said Sal. 'Nothing to it.' She got bored as Bill told them how to stand and hold the bow. In fact she did not listen at all. They lined up.

'One foot either side of the line.' A white tape marked the shooting line. 'Stand at right angles to it. Look straight ahead, arms outstretched level with your shoulders. Turn your head to the left, point your arm at the target. Got it?'

'Yes, sir.'

'Right, we'll try it now with arrows. Fit the notch, it's called the nock, into this bit here, the nocking point.'

Bill went along the line, getting the arrows in place. 'Place your fingers on the string, and prepare to address the target.'

'Ninety six, Muldoon Avenue,' giggled Sal, only to stop abruptly as Bill looked at her.

'Pull the bowstring back, that's right, back some more. I know you want to stop, but keep on pulling. Now when you're ready, let go.'

Six arrows left their bows. Tag's and Cowboy's headed towards the targets with the accuracy of cruise missiles. Narrinder's shot upwards into the sky and returned a few feet in front of her. Vicki's careered off wildly across the line of archers, while Brian seemed to have got himself in a knot. Sal's arrow had landed behind her. She had not been concentrating and had put her arrow backwards, with the flight feathers totally the wrong way round.

'Not bad,' said Bill.

'Blooming awful,' said Brian, but Bill sorted him out. Brian was left-handed so he had to do everything the opposite way to the others. No wonder he had got into such a tangle.

They spent ages practising. They each shot five arrows which they had to retrieve. Occasionally they had the joyful experience of gently pulling them out of the target. Usually they were stuck in the grass.

'I know what the sheets are for, Bill,' volunteered Tag. 'It's to stop the arrows going miles when you miss the targets. They sort of bounce off.'

Again and again they lined up. Narrinder was missing. She was found way beyond her target. Somehow one of her arrows had managed to speed through a hole in the sheet and she was searching for it. The others helped and then it was back to practice.

Sal was determined to do it. The harder she tried, the worse she was.

'Relax. You're too tense.' Bill was patient with her.

'Take your time.'

In exasperation Sal eyed up the target and released the bowstring with all the force at her command.

'Aw-yeoll,' she galloped off round and round in circles, screeching and yelling, before collapsing in a heap on the short grass, rolling and kicking. The others congregated around her.

'My arm! It's broken! I'm dying.' The bowstring had caught the soft flesh of her inner arm, twanging it harshly.

'Be a bit of a bruise,' said Bill, who had seen it all before. 'Come on, another go.'

Muttering dire threats under her breath, Sal returned to the line. Archery was stupid, Bill was a wally, the gang pathetic. It was all Miss Winter's fault. She knew Sal wanted to go canoeing. She'd get this arrow into the target if she had to stay here all day. The temptation to aim it at Bill was very strong. She could imagine the headlines. 'Bully Bill shot by girl archer'. She could pretend it was a mistake. Everyone would believe her. Something inside her calmed her down a bit and at last an arrow hit the outside white ring of the target.

'Well done,' said Bill, who decided it would be wise to ignore the fact that it was not her own target she had hit, but Narrinder's, which was next to hers.

'I've done it!' Brian was charging off across the field. 'A bull's nose.'

'Bullseye!'

'Brian, come back! Stop!' In his excitement Brian had forgotten the first rule of archery. Never retrieve your arrows while others are still shooting. He carried on oblivious of the missiles around him, still yelling, 'I've done it!' like a demented cat.

After that Bill called the lesson to a halt. It was funny, thought Sal, he looked a lot older than when they had first seen him.

'Well done,' he said, trying to encourage them. 'I want

us all to remember one thing.'

'Yes, Bill.'

'A bow is a lethal weapon and under no circumstances must it be considered a toy.'

'Yes, Bill,' and the gang drifted off back to the main buildings.

'Never did get to be an Indian,' said Cowboy.

'It was harder than it looked.' Vicki's understatement summed up the afternoon. At least she had managed to be on target half the time, thought Sal. All Sal had managed was one arrow on white and an aching arm.

Still, thought Sal, she would be ace at the other things. Sure to be. Anyway you can't be good at everything, people said, though she wasn't sure why not.

Just before tea, the class had to assemble in the dining room.

'Well, I can see that we have all had a great time.' Miss Winter looked pretty, her cheeks pink from being outside and her highlighted hair curled damply across her forehead. The red and white track suit looked good on her and made a change from the smart outfits she wore to school.

'Bill and Kevin want to have a talk to us all.'

Sal groaned. What if Bill told them all that she was hopeless? She glared at him, willing him to say nothing about her.

'Well, chaps, had your first activities. Good?'

'Yes.'

'You bet.'

'Should have seen Miss Winter on the death slide!'

'And Mr Rogers on the Canadian canoes.'

'We pushed him in.'

'And I fell in,' said Peter. 'In the lake.'

'We all did,' shouted the rest of his group.

Sal wished she could have been falling in lakes all afternoon. Sounded great fun.

'Chaps,' barked Bill. 'Listen!' Silence descended. 'A

few ground rules. Wet clothes in the drying room. No shoes in the dorms. Leave them on the low shelves in the hallway. Tuck shop open after meals. No food or drink in dorms. And remember, boys, stay in your dorm, girls in yours.' He turned to Kevin. 'Anything else?'

Kevin was still wearing his ridiculous hat. It had got wet and the top was bent over, almost hanging to his shoulder.

'You can go more or less anywhere but you must have a member of staff with you by the lake or river. Also don't feed the horses. They're not ours so keep away. You can stroke the donkeys, though.'

'Haven't seen them,' said Sal, quietly to Rachel.

'By the lake. They're lovely,' Rachel informed her.

'Also, you might have seen the fox cubs. We are rearing them to put back in the wild. Their mother was killed. You can look at them, but don't touch, okay?'

The gang looked at Sal who, with practised ease, put on her angelic expression. If they kept staring at her they would give the game away.

'So we want you all to enjoy yourselves. Any mischief and you get roped in to help the kitchen staff. Any questions?'

Brian's hand shot up. 'Where did you get that hat?'

'Ah, that would be telling. And there is a prize for whoever can capture it without violence, by the end of your visit.' Kevin paused and turned to Tag whose hand was waving in the air.

'I'm starving!'

This was the signal to set the tables and to attack the mountain of mashed potato, sausage and beans. Sal was ravenous. She had eaten hardly any lunch, because of the cub up her jumper. Narrinder played with her potato, making a ski run out of it, until Sal finished it for her.

All the children swopped stories of what they had been doing. As the meal ended everyone leapt up.

'Not so fast!' called Miss Winter. 'Sit down, everyone.' She handed them all an exercise book. 'After tea each night, we'll spend half an hour writing up our diaries.

'Aw, Miss.'

'Come off it!'

'This will remind you of what you have done,' she continued.

'I'll never forget Peter pushing me in the lake.'

'Or you screaming on the slide.'

'What *you've* done,' repeated the teacher. 'You can write, do pictures, whatever you like. So get started.'

Sal knew when to accept the inevitable. She jotted down a few things and let her mind wander while she drew herself doing archery. All her arrows were on target.

This camp was good fun, but she had not realised that she would have to do some things she did not like, such as archery and writing this stupid diary. That was the trouble with teachers. They always took the fun out of things by making you work. They couldn't just let you get on and enjoy everything.

Even on holiday you had to do some things you did not want to do. Sal wondered whether that was fair.

Hold on a minute, she thought. What was it she had learned about over the last few months. Things were often not fair, but it was how she reacted to them that mattered. Her new found friend Jesus would help her not to make a fuss or cause trouble. In all the excitement and activity of today she had forgotten to talk to him.

As she coloured in the archery field, she silently talked to Jesus. 'Hello, thanks for today. Help me not to make a fuss about the diary, and archery, and I'd really like it if I was good at the other things. Thank you for the lovely fox cubs and please stop me borrowing them again. Bye, for now.' And Sal jumped up, determined to make the most of the evening that lay ahead.

4

They were free to do what they liked all evening. Sal's gang headed straight for the archery field and most of the class joined them for a game of football.

It was a shame the stream trickled through the field as it got in the way of the game. There were no white lines or goal posts and the aim seemed to be to get the ball to the opposition's end of the field. This meant crossing the water.

By now the class was in roughly two halves, Sal's lot versus Tom's gang. All the rules of football were forgotten.

'Brian, Tag, guard the bridge and pipe, stop them crossing. Nar, you run with it,' ordered Sal. 'I'll fight them off.'

'Run with it? But I thought you could only kick in football.' Narrinder was not used to charging around like this.

'Just run,' and Sal made a mighty rugby tackle on Peter Wilkins, flooring him with a great show of strength.

Sitting on top of him, she grabbed the ball. 'Run!' she yelled at Narrinder. 'And you, Peter Wilkins, don't let me ever hear you say that girls are no good at football.'

'This isn't football. It's wrestling,' said Peter, wriggling helplessly like a trapped animal, 'or rugby.' But Sal was off.

Tag had got muddled up. He had stopped Narrinder crossing the bridge and she had not protested.

'Tag, you moron, she's on our side!' Sal screeched, as the opposition came herding towards her.

A glorious scuffle broke out on the bridge which was only a few boards loosely held together. Sal and Peter got wet for the second time that day. Tom and Simon settled an old disagreement by having a good punch up and Brian kept on telling everyone that this was not in the Football Association's rules and regulations.

The game continued. One or two of the quieter children sat on the grass calling out encouragement.

'Go on, Tag, kill him!'

'Push her in, Sal!'

Rugby scrum followed rugby scrum. Someone started throwing muddy clumps of grass into the fray until almost everyone was smeared and smelly.

Vicki who was wearing a clean white dress, walked up to the forgotten ball. Holding it at arm's length so as not to get dirty, she walked across the stream, where the battle still raged, and down to the far end of the field. There she put the ball into the fork of a tree and waited.

Sal emerged from under her scrum, green eyes alight, filthy and happy.

'Where's the ball?'

'The ball?'

It was nearly dark and in the fading light Vicki watched them hunt for the trophy.

'I've got it,' she called at last. 'We've won. It's in the tree.'

A one-nil victory was declared and everyone reckoned it was the best game of football they had ever had.

'Same time tomorrow,' challenged Tom, as they hung up more clothes in the drying room.

'You bet! We'll beat you ten-nil.'

Mrs Rowbottom overheard this exchange and the staff decided that someone had better supervise evening activities after tonight's escapade.

Most of the class, plus staff, drifted into the games

room. Here David Rogers was in his element.

'How about some tournaments? Snooker, table-tennis? Or board games for those of you who are less energetic?' He was wearing another pair of tatty jeans and his thick curly hair was plastered to his head as he had just washed it.

'Where's Miss?' asked Vicki.

'Here in a minute.'

'Do you love her lots and lots?'

'What do you think?' asked Mr Rogers.

'Will she still be our teacher when you are married?'

'Course. No life of leisure for a curate's wife,' replied Mr Rogers.

'Can we come to the wedding?' Narrinder queried.

'Should think so. It's just before Christmas. At the church.'

'Great!' and Narrinder sat down to discuss with Vicki what they would wear to their teacher's wedding. They were well into the details of what Miss should wear, the sort of reception she should have, how much money curates earned, and how to make the dirty stone church look nicer, when Miss Winter returned.

'I think I've just invited the class to our wedding,' David confessed, as Miss Winter collapsed into a saggy bottomed armchair.

Miss Winter just looked at him, lost for words. 'Well,' she said eventually, 'it had better be a buffet in the church hall.'

Civilised warfare broke out on the snooker table. No-one could remember how to score and the white ball went into the pockets as often as the red. Cues were waved dangerously around and peace was only restored when Mr Rogers invented his own scoring system and insisted that everybody stuck by it.

Sal was playing table tennis with Brian. The ping pong ball bounced off the walls, chairs and backs of people's heads, but the game continued.

'I've won,' declared Sal. 'Twenty-one to eighteen.'

'Rubbish. We're even.' But Sal had put her bat down and was now testing the armchairs.

When the seat cushions were removed, they revealed big baggy holes where the springs had given up. If you sat in the holes, it was as if the chair folded up around you and gave you a good cuddle. An impromptu game of musical chairs, without the music, took place.

Two or three children squashed, laughing, into one chair, the winner being the person whose backside was the most firmly wedged in the hole. Tag, tall and well built, was the obvious winner. Once he was stuck, no-one could shift him.

'Time for Operation Bed,' said Mr Wilkins, glancing at the clock. 'I'll be glad to see the back of you lot for a few hours.' He stood up. 'Bedtime!'

'Oh, no.'

'Bit longer.'

'Come on, sir!'

'I've said it, bedtime. Lights out at nine.' Mr Wilkins was insistent.

'Nine o'clock! You must be joking!' called Sal.

'No protests. Bathroom and bed.' Mr Wilkins marched the boys off and the girls were fussed over by Mrs Rowbottom. Apart from unsuccessfully trying to stop a game of 'let's see who can spit the farthest while doing their teeth', the thirty children were dispatched to their dorms. Hopefully to bed, hopefully to sleep.

'Night, Miss,' called Sal, sitting up in her bunk bed on the far side of the dorm.

'Goodnight, girls. Settle down quickly. You've had a busy day,' said Miss Winter.

'Yes, Miss,' came the joint reply.

As soon as she had shut the door the fun and games began. Sal felt trapped inside her sleeping bag. Her mum had bought her new pyjamas especially for camp. The legs wriggled up around her thighs and the top twisted so much that she felt as if she were tied up. After tugging at the zip, she found herself totally encased in the soft blue material of her sleeping bag.

'Hey, Vicki,' she called to the next bunk, 'I'm a caterpillar. Look!' Sal humped herself up and down her mattress, making the bunks sway wildly.

Gradually more and more girls joined in, unsuccessfully trying not to giggle.

'I'm a beautiful butterfly caterpillar,' said Narrinder, 'with red wings and white spots.'

'Sounds more like a toadstool,' commented Rachel, before she crashed over the end of her bed onto the floor. The combination of not wearing her thick glasses and the greeny-grey darkness meant that she was as blind as a bat. At least bats had a sort of radar to work out where they were going.

'Hey, I've got an idea,' said the crumpled heap on the floor. 'Let's have a caterpillar race.'

'Winner gets a lettuce!' shouted Marie.

Sal slithered to the floor. 'There's only space for two or three of us at a time.' As usual she was organising everyone. 'Me and Rachel and Narrinder will go first.'

Narrinder hesitated. 'Perhaps, well, it might not be a good idea. We're supposed to be in bed.'

'Chicken!' Sal challenged her. 'Anyway, we *are* in bed. Well, we're in the bags.'

Vicki lined them up and after Rachel found her glasses, they were off. The rest of the girls hung over their bunks cheering them on in loud whispers. Rachel looked so funny. A gleam of light reflected on her glasses and as her sleeping bag had brown and yellow stripes, she really did look like an oversized caterpillar. Narrinder was hardly making any effort, unlike Sal.

Got to win, thought Sal. I know, I'll go on my back, like backstroke swimming, be faster that way.

It was certainly faster but she could not keep in a straight line and bumped painfully into bed legs. Arriving at the door, she flipped over and pushed off with all the strength her feet could muster.

A shaft of bright electric light cut across the room. There, trapped in its beam, like moths, were the three contenders in the caterpillar race.

'What on earth . . . ?' Mrs Rowbottom did not look pleased.

'I fell out of bed,' explained Rachel, 'because of my glasses.'

'Your glasses?' Mrs Rowbottom could not make sense of what she was saying.

'So we helped her,' improvised Sal.

'In your sleeping bags?' asked the secretary.

'It was easier to stay in than to get out,' Sal said.

'Well you obviously found them,' said Mrs Rowbottom, pointing to the glasses perched on Rachel's head. 'Back to bed the lot of you, and be quiet.'

Silence reigned for three whole minutes.

'Do you think she believed us?' Narrinder whispered across the gap to Sal's bed.

'Course. What shall we do now?' replied Sal.

'Nothing. Go to sleep.'

'Can't. I'm not tired.' Sal paused, her brain ticking away. 'Got it!'

'Got what?' asked Vicki.

'We'll play pirates off ground.'

'But we'll get caught,' protested Narrinder.

'Not if we don't talk. Who's playing?'

The fifteen girls wriggled out of their bags. By now their eyes were accustomed to the dim light. The bunks made blocks of black shape and each girl was like a dark silhouette. Someone drew back the curtains, letting a pallid moonlight into the room. It made silvery paths across the floor.

'Right, I'm on,' said Sal. 'You're out if you touch the floor or if I catch you. I'll count to twenty and then you've had it.'

It was ace, jumping between the bunks, slithering across the gaps, trying to hide in dark corners. Quickly Sal caught a relieved Narrinder and blinky-eyed Rachel and then pounced on most of the others. In the end there was only Vicki to catch.

Sal's shadow was huge against the moonlit wall. It menaced down on Vicki who skilfully avoided it. By now the order to be quiet had been forgotten. The rest of the girls divided into two camps chanting either Sal or Vicki's name.

With great agility Vicki leapt across the wide gap between the two rows of bunk beds. Grinning like the Cheshire Cat in Alice in Wonderland, Vicki turned to face Sal. She crouched down on the bunk.

'Can't get me! Can't get me!' Vicki's long legs assured her of victory.

'You bet! Watch!' The trouble was that Sal could not take a running leap off the top bunk or she would hit her head on the ceiling. She prepared to pounce, copying the cats she had seen. With a great roar, like a lion, she sprang. Up and up . . . and down. Her hands flailed wildly and just grasped the cold metal bar at the end of the opposite top bunk. The impact made her lose her grip.

'Eeow!' she yelled, falling flat on her back on the floor. The world spun round and Sal was aware of a deathly hush.

Opening her eyes, she saw a green towelling dressing gown. She followed the folds upwards, past the bunched in belt, up and to the face smeared in cream looming down over her.

'Still looking for glasses?' asked Mrs Rowbottom.

Sal kept quiet.

'You know, Miss Winter and I are only next door. We expect some chatting, you know. *Chatting*, not leaping around like demented monkeys.'

'She was a lion, Miss,' said Marie.

'Or lions,' continued Mrs Rowbottom. 'It's now eleven o'clock. If there is any more noise from in here, there will be trouble. Understand?'

'Yes, Mrs Rowbottom,' they all said slowly.

Sal was helped to her feet. She was sure that she had broken her back. Her skinny bottom bones were aching from being a caterpillar and her archery-damaged arm was developing a pale bruise. She wondered if she would survive this camp. If she got any more injuries, she could sue them for damages. Hundreds of millions of pounds.

'Vicki,' she whispered, after she had fought her way into her sleeping bag. 'What would you do with millions of pounds?'

'Shut up and go to sleep.'

'Well, I'd go to Disneyland, buy a tropical island, have ten fox cubs, my own canoe. Could have my own lake. I could buy as many Mars bars as I could eat. I could buy the factory.' Sal paused. 'Are you listening?'

'No.'

'It's good here, isn't it?'

'Mmm.'

'Are you going to help me get Kevin's hat?'

'Mmm.' Vicki was nearly asleep.

'We'll have to think how to do it. I know.' Sal reached over and prodded her reluctant friend. 'We'll go now. He'll be asleep. We can pinch it.'

'Don't be so daft. I'm not going anywhere.'

Sal gave up. Why waste time going to sleep! There was so much to do here. Her mind trailed lazily over the events of the day. This morning seemed years away. She felt really happy, even if she was stiff.

Rolling over onto her side, she said her night time prayers, adding Foxy to the list of people she wanted God to look after. And without realising it she drifted off to sleep.

5

A terrible ringing, clanging noise blasted through the night, startling Sal. She put her head under the pillow but the awful din continued.

'Morning,' called Miss Winter, turning on the light.

'But I've only just gone to sleep,' said Sal.

'Probably true in your case,' said her teacher with a smile. 'It's seven o'clock. Rise and shine. Outside in ten minutes. Wear trainers for your run.'

'Run!' gasped Sal. 'I'm not running!'

'Ten minutes!' Miss Winter left the groaning, moaning tangle of girls to get dressed.

Sal had rarely experienced 7:15 in the morning and certainly had never been for a run at that time. She shivered in the cool air. The sky was pale unbroken blue and the outlines of the trees stood out sharply. Kevin and Bill led the straggling children in a gentle jog right round Greenlands. Automatically their feet obeyed their fuddled brains. Up, down, plod, plod.

By the look of them the boys had slept no better than the girls.

'No-one told me about that,' said Cowboy, as he collapsed at the breakfast table. 'What's this stuff?'

'Porridge,' said Vicki. 'It's got lots of fibre and prevents heart disease.'

'I think I'm going to have a heart attack.' Tag was the last to join them and insisted they all felt his pounding chest. 'I'm going to die!'

Whilst dying, he attacked his porridge. It had cooled and solidified.

'Looks like concrete,' said Tag.

'It is,' said Sal, and she took his bowl from him. 'Watch.'

While the gang crowded round her she swiftly turned the bowl upside down on a plate.

'It's a sandcastle,' she said. Tag's unyielding porridge stayed there while he filled up on unlimited supplies of toast and marmalade.

'Groups One and Two on kitchen duties,' called Miss Winter, as she came to tell them of the morning's activities. Sal's gang were to go with Kevin to the river to try Canadian canoeing.

They followed Kevin down past the lake to the river. It was quite wide but Kevin assured them that it was not deep. The grass grew all the way to the bank and lying there were three enormous canoes.

'Bags the middle one,' said Sal.

'Hang on, young lady, not so fast.' Kevin was joined by Mr Rogers and a woman they had not seen before. She was short and slim with spiky blonde hair. She wore a pink and purple wetsuit.

'This is Lisa, one of our water instructors. Now let's kit you out.' Kevin turned to Mr Rogers. 'They can all swim twenty-five metres? Good.'

Each of the gang was trussed in bright orange lifejackets. Sal felt like a stuffed turkey in hers, the front ballooning over her chest. She could not even see her feet squeezed into her oldest tattiest trainers.

'We're going to have three of us in a canoe,' said Kevin. 'One instructor and two of you. Mixed pairs, I think. Now who knows what these are?'

'Canoes.' Brian stated the obvious.

'Canadian canoes. Originally made of birch bark by North American Indians; these are fibreglass. The best way to learn is to do it, so follow me.'

Sal was with Brian and Mr Rogers. They picked up the surprisingly light canoe and walked into the cold water that numbed their legs.

Getting in was the first problem. Narrinder and Tag misjudged their entry, capsized the canoe and ended up spluttering in the slow moving water. It was hard to walk on the muddy river bottom, squelching along as if wearing concrete boots. At last they were all in.

The instructors passed them all a paddle. The pale brown wooden poles felt very awkward to handle.

'Right. Lisa, Mr Rogers and I will steer, until you get the hang of it. Dip your paddles in gently, pull, glide and in again.' Kevin demonstrated. 'We need a rhythm so all repeat after me, "chocolate biscuits".'

'Chocolate biscuits.'

'Dip your paddles in on "choc" each time. You'll soon get the hang of it.'

They all tried. The three canoes seemed to have a will of their own. Sal was squashed between Brian and Mr Rogers. "Chocolate biscuits" they chanted, but it did not help. Mr Rogers showed them both how to exert the same amount of pressure on the paddles and suddenly they were doing it.

'We'll all have a practice run. Follow me.'

Like magic the three craft glided down the river. It was ace. They all got splashed, sometimes paddles got tangled up, but they were moving.

'Turn!' called Kevin from the leading canoe. 'All dip your paddles to the left, lean forward and work hard.'

Sal was astonished when her canoe faced the opposite way. They had to wait a bit while Narrinder, soaked for the second time, was retrieved. She had leaned too far forward and shot out of the canoe.

Up and down they cruised, growing in confidence, arms and shoulders aching.

'Time for a race,' said Kevin. 'To the bridge.'

The three canoes wobbled along, more or less level. To Sal's amazement, Brian stopped paddling. Calmly he removed his glasses, oblivious of the fact that his paddle was drifting away.

'Brian, are you all right?' Mr Rogers was concerned.

'Yes, sir. It's my glasses. They got all wet and I can't see where I'm going.' And Brian carried on wiping them with the bottom of his T-shirt.

Sal was furious. Poking him in the back she hissed, 'Get a move on, you wally. We're last.'

'But I couldn't see.'

'I don't care. You didn't need to see. Here, I'll get your paddle.'

Sal tried to grab it, missed, fell out and capsized the canoe. Brian seemed to think it was funny. Sal was livid.

'Now look what you've done. We've sunk.' The life-jacket bobbed her around in the water making her feel like a hunchback.

'Hey, Sal, calm down.' Mr Rogers was draining the water out of the canoe. 'It was an accident.'

'His stupid fault, more like.'

'Come on, Sal, it's only fun. Now get back in,' said Mr Rogers. 'I don't think anger is one of the things that Jesus likes in his followers,' he added quietly, so only she could hear.

Sal fell silent. All right for Mr Rogers to say that but it was *her* that was mad, not him. And anyone would be right to be angry if they were paired with a useless twit like Brian.

Her bad mood evaporated as they joined the others and were taught to rock the canoe and stand up in it without capsizing. Of course they all fell in lots of times.

'See why you were told to bring plenty of old clothes?' said Mr Rogers, as once again they peeled off their stuff in the drying room.

Sal grinned. The room smelt awful. Its aim was to dry off dirty, not clean, clothes, and the smell of old mud and stale sweat hung in the warm damp air.

'Bet we're back in here again today,' said Mr Rogers. 'Raft building after break. All of you.'

'Great!' said Sal. She would have been happy to stay in her wet clingy clothes all the time and save the bother of changing.

When they returned to the side of the river, the grass was piled high with equipment – giant oil barrels, coiled snakes of rope and lots of roughly sawn logs. Each group was to make its own raft and later they would launch them. All the staff and instructors were there to help. Mostly they got in the way.

Bill showed them how to do square lashing, tying the planks together with reef and granny knots. It looked dead easy. All they had to do was fix four or six barrels together and put the planks on top.

Sal took charge. 'Right, we'll have one barrel each. On its side, Narrinder. Honestly, you're hopeless.'

'I don't like to keep getting wet,' said Narrinder, her plaits still damp from earlier that morning.

'And I'm fed up with getting dirty,' complained Vicki.

'Well, just stay dirty and only get changed if you are wet,' said Sal.

'I can't.' Vicki was half-way through her second suitcase and there were still two days left.

Sal ignored them. 'Tie the barrels together.'

It was easier said than done. The old black metal barrels rolled away. Cowboy was messing around, balancing on his, like a performing sea-lion. Quietly Brian fetched Lisa, the instructor, who helped them. The planks were laid ready for tying. Lisa did the first knot, her agile fingers moving quickly, and then she went to help another group.

Square knotting was not difficult if done slowly. Sal wanted them to hurry up. Narrinder gave up and watched a party of ducks playing in the water. Sal got cross. Her piece of rope was too short and in temper she flung it into the water where it floated like a pale eel.

'Look, like this.' Brian was standing on the raft, bent

double, a neat row of knots showing his handiwork. He stepped backwards and jerked over, moaning softly, his right foot seemingly trapped, his glasses hanging over his ears.

'You daft bat,' said Lisa kindly. 'You've tied the lace of your trainer in with the rope.' She turned to the gang. 'This is a great exercise for learning to work together well. I bet that the best raft will be the one where the team consulted each other.'

Consult this lot! thought Sal. Lisa must be joking. The only way their raft would float was if they did what *she* told them.

'Stop bossing us about,' said Cowboy, who had been quite happy working on his bit, until Sal moved in. 'I know what I'm doing.'

'Well, I don't know what you're doing.'

'So?'

'So, do that bit there.'

'Forget it,' Cowboy carried on while Narrinder, anxious to avoid a scene, came over to help.

Sal was getting increasingly impatient. Some of the other rafts were finished. Theirs looked a mess. Pride prevented her from asking an adult for help. She made a flag out of a long twig and Tag's T-shirt and stuck it in a gap between the planks. That made it look a lot better.

'Before we launch,' called Kevin, 'all put your life-jackets on. Then stand by your raft.'

Big waxy crayons were passed to each group.

'These are face paints. You're Red Indians, so decorate yourselves up.'

They looked fantastic. Stripes and circles, splodges and dots, in all colours. Cowboy decorated Brian and Tag's bare chests with skull and crossbones while Sal traced one of her veins up her leg with fat purple dots.

'Now the war cry!' Kevin led the colourful savages in what he said was a Rain Dance. Even Mrs Rowbottom joined in. She looked so funny in ancient khaki shorts, her life-jacket bobbing up and down and a red sun and moon painted on her cheeks.

'To the launch, and may God bless all who sail in her.'

Each group, with an instructor, heaved their raft into the water. All made it and the warriors scrambled aboard as best they could. Kevin waded among them handing out paddles.

'Right, steer right!' yelled Sal, standing up, wobbling on her raft.

The raft ploughed straight ahead.

'To the right!'

It rammed the far bank with such force that Sal was jolted off the back into the still water. She didn't mind. It was great fun.

By now, the raft made by Peter's team had come adrift.

'Abandon ship!' called his instructor, Bill. 'Man the lifeboats.' The raft disintegrated and the team held onto barrels and planks, as they all laughed and splashed.

'Sink the enemy!' screeched Bill, as with great gusto he urged his troops on. Marie's raft was upended, depositing them all in the water, and Bill approached Sal's raft.

'Splash!' yelled Sal. 'He thinks he's in the war.'

'Thought he was army, not navy,' said Brian, who liked to get his facts right.

They had a wonderful battle. How Sal held out for so long with such pathetic troops, she never knew. Cowboy was okay, splashing and yelling away and Brian would have been all right if he could have seen what he was doing. Without his glasses, now safely on shore, he splashed Sal as much as the enemy. Tag had to be told what to do, but at least he was big and useful for pushing invaders off the raft. But the girls! Hopeless. Narrinder soaked to the skin and trying not to get wetter. And

Vicki prancing round like a right ninny, squealing when spots of muddy water splashed her.

Sal realised that her gang were okay at school, were pretty good as friends, but were hopeless when it came to the really important things in life – like winning the battle of the rafts. Mixed in with her great enthusiasm was a growing annoyance at the others. If there had been six of them like her, they would have won. As it was, the raft was soon demolished.

It took ages to rescue all the planks and barrels from the water. Tag's T-shirt was never seen again. Sal tried to ride on a barrel, legs astride, like a horse, but even with the help of the others, she kept falling off. At last, soaked, happy, exhausted and starving they crawled out onto the bank.

'That was ace,' said Sal to Lisa. 'What's happening to Mr Rogers?'

'He escaped so he has to be ducked.'

The children cheered and whistled as a clean dry Mr Rogers was carried kicking and yelling down to the water's edge by Kevin and Bill. Miss Winter was laughing as her future husband was drenched, fully clothed, in the river.

'Next time, you're first in,' said Bill, pretending to be stern.

'Won't be a next time. Angela, how did you manage to rope me in to help with this lot?' His gaze took in the massed wet children with coloured warpaint still smudged over their faces. 'I must be mad!'

'You are,' called someone, as they drifted off to get washed and changed. The drying room was nearly full of flapping soggy clothes that smacked them in the face.

Sal had had an ace morning. The only thing that had spoilt it was getting cross. I wish I didn't, she thought, but it's not my fault. They're so daft. Brian and his glasses, Vicki and Narrinder messing around. It's all right the Bible saying not to get angry and that, but I bet they didn't have people like Brian around in those days. I wonder, her mind side-tracked, whether they had rafts and canoes. Probably proper fishing boats, and she went off to lunch, pretending that she was a fisherman in the time of Jesus.

6

After a huge late lunch of yet more sandwiches and soup it was time for the afternoon's activities. Down near the lake was the assault course. The lake was egg shaped and in the middle was an island covered in scrubby bushes and spiky trees. The island was joined to the shore by a metal walkway.

On one corner of the island there was a bare patch. This was the landing place for a long rope swing. Across the entire lake and island was another stronger rope, its end disappearing mysteriously into the trees. The death slide!

'Sir, me, Bill, sir!' Sal was leaping up and down. 'I'll go first.'

'Any other volunteers?' Bill looked round at the team. 'Okay, Sal, you can be our pioneer.'

'It's very high,' said Narrinder.

'I'm not doing it.' Tag was adamant.

'They all say that,' Bill told him, 'but they all do it.'

'Well, I won't,' muttered Tag under his breath.

The slide started halfway up a tree. Sal slowly clambered up the wooden planks nailed onto the trunk, higher and higher, her eyes fixed on Bill's boots just above her. She could feel the rough wood under her fingertips and her pumps, with the holes in, slid on the ladder. Her heart seemed to be going faster than normal. Usually she was not even aware that it existed. Now something was bump-bumping away under her jumper.

Bill helped her onto the platform. Sal gulped. It was so high up! She could see right across Greenlands which looked like a model below her. Looking up, she noticed how bare the huge tree branches were. Then she glanced down, definitely a mistake. Four pale faces plus one brown one were upturned watching her.

Fastening her into a harness, Bill gave Sal instructions.

'You can't fall. The harness will stop you. Put your wrists through this loop above your head.' Sal's arms would not obey his commands so Bill looped them through the leather thong. 'See it tightens. Now all you have to do is leap off. Take a running jump if you like.'

Leap off! He must be mad. The death slide stretched out forever. She would never cross all that water, the island, and land safely on the other side.

'Go on, Sal,' called Brian, urging her on. 'My turn next.'

Sal shut her eyes and leapt out to certain death. No wonder it was called the death slide. Her arms jolted as the rope took her weight. Squinting her eyes open, Sal felt a marvellous mix of fear and excitement.

I'm flying, she thought, gliding across the lake. It's brill. She was enjoying her fear and made sure she looked straight ahead and not down. Not realising that she was screaming out loud, her feet brushed the top of the island's trees.

'Enemy parachute landing! Weee!'

The slide dipped down, her feet skimming the lake before rising over the bank. A few more seconds and Sal slowed to a halt, her rope bumping into an old tyre fastened to the slide.

'It was brill! I'm doing it again. Did you see me! Mr Wilkins, did you see me?'

Peter's dad smiled. 'Course. And heard you! Now keep still while I get this off.'

Released from the harness, Sal sprinted back to the others, bouncing in the air, punching her fists skyward.

'It's ace,' she told them.

'Why were you screaming then?' asked Tag.

'Well, you have to. Makes it more fun.'

While each one had their turn, the others played around on huge rope nets and climbed up and down trees. Sal was longing to have another go and Bill had said she could if there was time. Time seemed to be going very quickly.

'Get a move on, Tag,' Sal called to him. He had been on the platform for ages. What was he doing? Bird spotting or something?

'I'm not doing it.' Tag was terrified. No way was he jumping into space and no way was he coming back down the plank ladder.

'You'll be okay,' Narrinder tried to encourage him. Even she had been brave enough to try.

'It's fine,' said Brian. Well, it had been for him. Without his glasses he did not know whether he was two or twenty metres in the air.

'Can't,' said Tag, with what sounded suspiciously like a sob.

Sal turned away, disgusted, kicking a chunk of leaf mould angrily in front of her. What a baby! The biggest, strongest member of the gang and he was a right wimp. Her cheeks flushed with embarrassment. Tag, in the gang, no, in *her* gang, a cowardly chicken. She'd never live down the shame.

'Do it, you great soppy wally,' she yelled. 'I'll never forgive you, if you don't.'

'Sal, be quiet,' called Bill. 'Try to understand.'

'Understand! I understand, all right. He's useless. Yellow-belly, jelly-kneed, barmy.'

'Shut up,' Bill was down the tree, glaring at her fiercely. 'Can't you see he's upset?'

Tag was crying! Fat blobby tears streaming down his muddy face. Narrinder had her arm round his shaking body.

'I'm sss . . . sorry,' he said.

'It's okay, Tag. It doesn't matter,' said Narrinder.

'I was scared too,' said Cowboy.

'And me,' Brian confessed. Sal stomped over to the rope swing. Pushing off she swung, Tarzan-like, over the lake, well away from her team. Tag was the only person in the class, apart from Mrs Rowbottom, who had not been on the death slide. Even Miss Winter had done it. Sal would never forgive him. Moodily she swung backwards and forwards. The others conveniently ignored her as they involved Tag in a game of chase.

I'll try to reach the island, she thought, giving herself a big push off from the bank. Misjudging her landing, she splattered into the lake, bits of water weed sticking to her. She did not care, her bad mood getting worse. Sal just sat there until Bill told her to get out, get changed and stay over by the dorms.

'Can't I come back in a minute, to do the assault course?' she asked.

'No. I'm afraid that we cannot have bad tempered people in our troops.'

'But you *can* have cry babies!'

'Pardon?' said Bill.

'Aw, nothing.' Sal squelched off. 'Nuts to the lot of you.'

After a long shower, Sal got dressed. She was running out of clothes and had to wear one of her older brother's ripped T-shirts that Mum had insisted on packing. It hung down to her knees. She lay on her bunk, her hair wetting the rolled up sleeping bag.

It's not fair, she thought. I don't do nothing wrong and I've got to stay here. Tag's a wimp and he's treated like royalty. She lay there, enjoying her misery, feeding her anger with thoughts of all the daft things her gang had done at camp. They did not seem to try. Just messed about.

'Sal, are you there?'

Sal sat upright.

'I thought you might like a cup of tea. I heard you

got wet again.' Miss Winter padded quietly towards her.

'Thanks, Miss.'

'And what are you doing here?' she said. 'I thought it was assault course for your team. I thought you'd love that.'

'I do. Did. It's all Tag's fault. He wouldn't do it, and I couldn't have another go and Bill told me off.' Sal stared at the ceiling refusing to meet her teacher's gaze. Miss Winter rested her arms on the bunk.

'So it's Tag's fault?'

'Yes. He wouldn't do it and *I* got told off. It's not fair.'

'And why do you think you were told off?'

Sal was silent. She had not thought about why. As far as she could see she had not done anything wrong.

'I didn't do anything,' she began. 'Honestly.'

'Did you say anything, think anything?' Miss Winter was talking very softly. 'I rather think you got a bit cross.'

A bit cross! thought Sal. Flaming mad would be more accurate.

'How do you feel about that now?' continued Miss Winter.

'I suppose,' she said reluctantly. 'I suppose, I shouldn't. Get cross, I mean. But they make me so mad.'

'They make you?'

'Yes.'

'Actually, Sal. I think you make yourself mad. Today with Tag, yesterday with Brian.'

Trust Mr Rogers to tell her about that, thought Sal.

'It might help you, Sal, to think about love.'

'Love?' What was she on about?

'Yes. Loving others. I know that you want to follow Jesus, don't you?'

'Yes, Miss.'

'Well, he talked a lot about loving others. It's a mark, a sign, of being a Christian.' Miss Winter paused. 'And when we love others, we try not to get mad at them.'

'But I can't help it.'

'Why don't you have a think about it? When you get angry inside you could tell Jesus how you feel and then ask him to help you. You could try to stop thinking about being cross. Instead you could think about how to love the person you are mad at.'

'I'll never be able to do that,' Sal said. Loving someone who was driving you nuts?

'Course you won't,' Miss Winter said, surprising her. 'Not on your own. Not without God's help. You know, Sal, I'll tell you something.'

'What?'

'It makes me cross when people say it's nice and easy to be a Christian. There's nothing easy about loving others or nice about forgiving them.'

There was a comfortable silence.

'Anyway, enough of the serious stuff. Would you like a game of table-tennis until the others come back?'

'Thanks, Miss, but I'm a bit tired. I'll stay here.'

Sal lay dozing on the bed. It was not often that she was alone. Home was bursting with brothers, baby sister and children that Mum minded. After school she nearly always played with the gang. Being on her own was strange.

She could hear the distant sounds of children squealing, and pans clanging in the kitchen. Someone was cutting wood nearby, the power saw sizzling through the air. It was hot and she ached all over, especially her arms from the rope swing.

Love not anger. Sounded impossible. I mean, I could try to stop being cross, she thought, but to love them! Never, I'll never be able to do it. Anyway, how could I love Tag or Brian, or anyone who makes me mad?'

She thought of the stories she had heard at the youth group. They always had one at the end of the evening. A phrase crept into her mind. It was something that

Jesus had once said. "Love one another, as I have loved you". They even sang a song about it. Sal had never paid much attention to the words before – "as I have loved you".

'Well, Jesus,' she said out loud, 'you even died for people 'cos you loved them, and made them better and told them about God. And you want *me*, Sally Musgrove, to love people like you do. Wow!'

She paused. 'Well, then, you'll have to help me, cos I'll never do it and I'm not even sure it's worth trying. So will you? Help me, I mean?'

Drifting off to sleep, Sal felt warm and snug. Without even realising it, her anger had gone, though how long it would disappear for she did not know.

After tea, which had been a noisy affair, though not as rowdy as usual, because Sal was fairly quiet, Mr Rogers stood up.

'Are you full up!'

'Yes,' yelled everyone.

'So no-one's got room for hot-dogs?'

'Yes! Course!'

'It's camp-fire night. Everyone into your teams and we'll build a fire and have a feast.'

They pulled old logs and broken branches out of the assault wood and fetched bundles of twigs from the big wood at the far side of the archery field. It was hard work but fun. Soon they had constructed a huge bonfire, shaped like a wigwam.

It was getting cooler as darkness fell. The class collected anoraks and gloves and sat on old benches by the campfire.

Eventually Bill and Kevin lit the fire. The wood crackled and spat, small flames trickling upwards to be joined by others and form great tongues of fire. Sparks, orange and gold, flew upwards into the black night, whirling and twisting like disco dancers in a competition. Mysterious caves, full of blue and purple light, formed in the heart of the fire and charred twigs stretched out their gnarled hands into the bottomless caverns.

It seemed as if they sang every song they knew. Mr Rogers' guitar was drowned by the assorted voices bawling away about 'green bottles hanging on the wall', the fate of John Brown's body and falling from forty thousand feet.

Sal felt happy, singing her lungs out. The front of her body was glowing with the warmth of the fire. The heat seemed to spread inside her, melting away all her anger, and replacing it with a mushy sort of feeling. Was this what was meant by love?

She looked around at all her friends, dark huddled shapes with golden faces, stuffing hot dogs as if they had not eaten in days.

Sal got up, feeling the stiffness in her body, and walked over to Tag. She turned her back to the fire, glad that the darkness hid her face.

'Tag,' she said, tapping his shoulder. 'Tag, listen.'

'Emmm,' Tag's cheeks bulged with sausage, a trickle of tomato sauce, like blood, escaping from the corner of his mouth.

'I'm sorry I got so cross at you – on the death slide.' Sal said the words as quickly as she could.

'I couldn't help it,' Tag mumbled through his mouthful.

'I know. Anyway I'm sorry.'

'It's okay.' Tag paused and Sal wondered what was coming next. 'Do you want it?' He pointed to her half-eaten hot dog.

'No, I'm full up.' And friendly relationships were re-established as Tag vacuumed up the gang's left-overs.

Well, that wasn't too bad, thought Sal. If love was giving someone your supper, when you didn't want it yourself, it should not be too hard to do.

Her eyes suddenly glimpsed something. Green and

yellow. Striped. Bobbing about by the fire. Kevin's monstrous hat. This would be a good time to get it. Vicki had promised to help. But how would they do it?

7

Sal searched unsuccessfully for Vicki. Eventually Tag told her that she was down by the horses' field. Stumbling in the darkness, Sal found her, sitting on the fence talking to the animals.

'And we'll gallop away, over the fields, jump the hedges, on and on, and then we'll trot back.' Vicki was in a world of her own.

'Are you nuts or something?' asked Sal. 'Talking to horses?'

Vicki jolted out of her daydream. 'Oh, it's only you.'

'You said you'd help.'

'Help what?'

'Get it,' said Sal.

'Get what?'

'The hat. Honestly, Vicki, you don't listen.'

'I do when people talk sense.'

'We've got to get Kevin's hat. I've thought of a plan. You've got to help.' Sal was trying to get Vicki's full attention without going too near the horses.

'Forget it.'

'You promised. In the dorm. I asked you and you said "mmm".'

'Can't count that,' said Vicki.

'You *must*!'

Vicki was silent. A dream was beginning to form in her own mind. If she helped Sal, then Sal would owe her one. Sal would have to help her.

'I'll do it, if you help me.'

'Help you what?'

'It's a secret, but you've got to promise.' Vicki turned and in the moonlight Sal could see that she looked very determined.

'Okay then, but hurry up. The fire'll be out soon,' and the two girls rejoined the others.

'Kevin,' Vicki peered up at him. 'Can I ask you something?'

'Sure. What?'

'Can you sit down. It's easier to talk.' Kevin obliged by lowering his strong body onto a bench. 'It's about the canoes.'

'Yes.'

'Well . . . er . . . I wanted to know,' Vicki racked her brains. What on earth could she want to know? 'To know, about if you tip out.'

'Capsize, you mean. We showed you what to do.' He smiled and started to get up. Quickly Vicki pushed him down. Sal was not quite in position, creeping up behind him, her teeth glinting whitely in the dying firelight. Vicki had got to keep him talking. She put on her best smile while her brain whirled rapidly.

'No, I mean, say, well if you got stuck upside down and your legs were trapped.'

'Oh, I see. Well that's one of the reasons you should never canoe alone. There's a technique to rescue someone . . . what the heck?' Kevin jumped up but it was too late. The hat had gone, grasped by Sal.

Quickly she ran shouting, 'I've got it,' the hat perched on her head. It was enormous and slowly slid down her forehead over her eyes and across her nose. The stuck-on pink ears waggled like oversized handles.

'Could pick her up like a trophy,' said Mr Rogers, as she sped past him, with Kevin in hot pursuit.

'Stop him!' yelled Sal. Slowly the class got the idea and formed human obstacles in Kevin's way. He swatted them to one side, as if they were wasps, and jumped over them, pounding after his precious hat, which was on the far side of the fire.

Sal could hardly see where she was going. The itchy wool was like a green mesh in front of her eyes and she was unsure of her whereabouts. Like a wounded animal she fled blindly, zig-zagging and stumbling.

'Watch out!' It was Tag's voice. 'He's nearly got you.'

Strong fingers brushed her ankles in vain as Kevin launched himself in a flying rugby tackle. Missed! Sal tripped and rolled over and over, through something thick, sticky and smelly. Surely the horses had not been here!

Sal pulled the hat off so she could see better. She wished that she had not. A huge shiny face, split in two by a wicked grin, was bearing down on her. Two great hands on robot-like arms were about to pin her down.

'Vicki! Catch!' Sal made her last desperate move and flung the battered hat into the night air. Up it went, followed by the gaze of 4N, their hot-dog smeared hands reaching out to grab it.

They need not have bothered. The hat arched over, did a back flip, and gently, the hot air filling it like a balloon, dropped with deadly accuracy into the fire. Right in the middle. The glowing embers burst into life and a single golden flame licked upwards. It lit up the pink plastic ears grotesquely melting into revolting squirmy messes, before dying down again.

Sal shut her eyes. This was it! If she kept them shut she could pretend that she was not here.

Kevin's vice-like grip seized her middle. He spun her upwards and she landed on his shoulders. Firmly holding onto her legs, which hung round his neck like a tattered scarf, Kevin let out a war cry and galloped off.

Everyone cheered and yelled encouragement. Sal thought she would throw up, bouncing along, her arms clasped over Kevin's head. If this was what horse riding was like, you could forget it!

Kevin ground to a halt. 'What shall I do with her?'

Sal risked opening an eye. She looked down on her classmates. They were all laughing.

'To bed!'

'Shove her in the fire!' Sal hoped not!

'Make her clear up.'

'Get her to knit you a new hat.' Some hope, thought Sal.

'I know,' boomed Kevin, as his audience grew quieter. 'I'll give her the prize.'

'The prize!' shouted Brian.

'Well she got the hat, didn't she?' Kevin lowered Sal to the ground. 'I'll fetch it.' And he returned with a tiny box.

Opening it, Sal was amazed to see a miniature canoe carved out of wood.

'It's great,' she said, thanking him. 'I'll keep it forever. But what about the hat?'

'Plenty more where that came from,' said Kevin. 'Now, time for all to clear up and then it *is* bed.' A collective groan greeted this statement. 'And I don't want any mischief from you tonight. Understand?'

'Yes,' they all chorused, trying not to smile. Everything was ready for tonight's activities after lights out. In fact, thought Sal, as they quickly got ready for bed, the unofficial activities were as much fun as the ones Greenlands had prepared for them.

The quietness in the dormitories was unbelievable. The staff waited for ten minutes but nothing happened.

'I'm going over to the games room,' said Mr Rogers. 'Coming?'

'I'll just check the girls. They must all be exhausted to get off to sleep so quickly.' Miss Winter walked down the gap between the two rows of bunk beds, each containing an unmoving silent lump. 'Fast asleep,' she said as she and Mr Rogers walked across the courtyard to the games room to join the other staff.

Sal squinted through the gap in the curtains. 'All clear, they've gone.' It was the signal. From bags and under mattresses hoards of food were produced.

'What's that?' asked Vicki.

'It's from lunch. I took some extra sandwiches.' Rachel pointed to the squashed pile of bread.

'Looks revolting. Where's the pop?'

'I've got it.' Marie clanked towards the far end of the room. They had spread some sleeping bags on the floor and were squatting on them.

'When are the boys coming?'

'Twelve,' said Sal.

'That's ages,' complained Marie.

'Well,' said Sal slowly. 'You can't have a midnight feast before midnight, otherwise it would be a half-past ten feast.'

'Or a three minutes to eleven feast.'

'Sal,' said Narrinder. 'Come here a minute.' Sal followed her back to the bunks. 'Do you think we should? Have the feast, I mean. That Bill said no food in the dorms. And no boys in here, either.'

'They'll never know, and anyway he didn't mean it.'

'But,' Narrinder was worried, 'we'll get into trouble.'

'Don't worry.' Sal went back to the others. Perhaps her friend was right. Perhaps they should not do it. But it had been her idea. She could hardly call it off now. The others would think she had gone mad or something. Trouble was she had forgotten all about the no food rule until Narrinder had reminded her. Well she would just have to forget about it again.

It seemed like hours before the boys came in. Brian had a torch and led the way, tripping over his long pyjamas.

'Tom and Simon are asleep,' he said disgustedly, 'and I can't wake them up.'

The boys' offerings were added to the pile of food. The tuck shop had obviously done good business today.

Remembering to keep the noise down, they attacked the food. They had a competition to see whose crisp soaked in pop would stay in one piece the longest. Soon the floor was littered with pink fragments that looked like confetti after it has rained.

'Let's have a bubble competition,' suggested Sal. 'Girls against boys. You have to get your bubbles all in the bottle and over the top.'

They found eight small bottles and carefully measured the same amounts of pop into each. The four boys and girls sat opposite each other, straws in mouths, the rest crowding around.

'Go!' said Marie.

Blowing and slurping, spluttering and puffing, burping and hiccuping . . . the race was on.

'It's gone down my nose,' whispered Cowboy, red stains spotting his pyjama top.

'Shut up and keep blowing.' Brian urged him on.

Eight columns of bubbles rose and poured over the sides. Forgetting it was a competition, they carried on. The bubbles joined together and tiny rivulets trickled over legs, into sleeping bags and onto the floor. Others joined in until the end of the room looked like a witch's cauldron with disgusting gulping noises producing red and orange coloured bubbles that collapsed upon themselves.

The rivulets joined to form a stream that flowed through the boulders of crisps and round the mountains of sandwiches. Sal flicked a piece of the soggy mess. It stuck on the wall before sliding slowly downwards, a pink slimy trail in its wake.

Sal wished she had not done it.

Everyone started flicking wet food. Peter managed to get some on the ceiling where it stayed. In a matter of seconds they were pelting each other with the remains of the midnight feast.

'Stop it!' Sal was grabbing them, but no-one took any

notice, except Narrinder who had crept back to bed.

'Please, stop it!' The class ignored her, food missiles flying everywhere. This was all going horribly wrong. The mess was revolting.

If only I hadn't had the idea for the feast, thought Sal. We'll be killed!

The only hope was to clear up the mess and get back to bed. That way no-one would know. Sal made one last effort.

'Stop it!' she screamed and instantly a hush descended.

'Stop what?'

Everyone looked. There, in the doorway, her cuddly dressing-gowned shape silhouetted by the light behind her, stood Mrs Rowbottom. As they watched she was joined by the rest of the staff. The lights went on. Twenty-eight children, most of them covered in red pop, sat in the middle of chaos. Lumps, unrecognisable, splattered the walls like bullet holes.

'I don't want to hear a word, not a word.' said Mrs Rowbottom, her eyes quickly taking in the scene. After telling them how irresponsible they were, she made them clean up.

It took ages to wipe down the walls, unstick the food bullets and tidy everything. The red pop had stained most of their night clothes and they had to change. Sal was given the job of putting all the night-clothes to soak in a bath of hot water and washing powder.

'I'll put them through a machine tomorrow,' said Mrs Rowbottom, as she passed the clothes to Sal. 'If this soak doesn't get the stains out, I don't know what will.' She turned to look at Sal. 'I honestly do not know what the matter is with you all. A bit of fun, yes, we expected that, but you lot are like savages. And who planned this escapade, I'd like to know.'

She gave Sal a knowing look. 'Auden Junior School will be banned from Greenlands if this carries on.'

Mrs Rowbottom moaned on and on. Sal was tired and thoughtful. She was reduced to sleeping in a dress of Vicki's. It had red and white stripes and was much too big for her. Sal felt like a circus tent in it.

It was not her fault that the feast had gone wild. Okay, so she'd had the idea, but if she had not thought of it, someone else would.

It wasn't really wrong, she thought. I mean, I can see that it was a *bit* wrong because we did what we were told not to do. But it was only a little thing, some food and pop. Sal realised that it did not matter that it was only a bit wrong. Wrong was wrong, full stop. She should not have done it.

Messed it up again, she thought. And I didn't mean to. It just happens. It's been an ace day and I've spoilt it. She felt sad as she crawled back to bed and as usual said her prayers.

'I'm sorry, Jesus, I didn't mean it. Please help me to stop doing things wrong.' Sal curled up in a tight ball. From now on she would make sure that she had lots of fun without getting into trouble. Like today, with Kevin's hat, that had been a real laugh, much more fun than the feast. And even though the hat had got burnt, she had not been told off because it was an accident.

'Yes,' she said to herself, as she fell asleep. 'I'm going to do just what I'm told!'

8

'Sally,' said Mrs Rowbottom at breakfast next morning. 'Your team are on kitchen duties.'

'Aw, Miss,' Sal began and stopped. What was it she had thought last night? Doing just what she was told. Well, here was the first test.

'Potato peeling for you,' Mrs Rowbottom continued. 'There's quite a big sack to get through.' She seemed pleased at the prospect.

Sal stood at the deep sink trying to wrestle with the potato peeler which seemed more intent on taking the skin off her hands than off the potatoes. She would be here for hours. Cowboy and Vicki helped while Narrinder and Tag sliced the potatoes into chip shapes.

'This one's like a duck,' said Cowboy, quickly carving eyes into the potato.

Sal rummaged through the sack. 'I'll make this one into a totem pole. Here, Narrinder, this one looks like your dad.'

Spud bashing forgotten they carved weird and wonderful shapes.

'Assault course in a quarter of an hour,' Bill's voice penetrated into the kitchen, 'for those who are ready.'

The gang worked like mad, hoping that no-one would examine the chips too closely before they fried them. Peel was everywhere and they hastily tidied up, conveniently kicking dropped bits under the sink.

'Troops assemble!' Bill obviously thought he was a sergeant major again. 'You horrible lot are next. The rest have done theirs.'

'Done their what?' asked Sal.

'Timed assault. All teams to complete the course. Fastest team wins. Peter's team in lead.' And Bill strode off to the wood. 'Practice first.'

Sal made for the rope net. It was huge and a bit like a ladder. The aim was to scramble up it, over the top and down the other side onto the next part of the course. She jumped on it and the waxy ropes swung all over the place, bouncing her around.

It was harder than it looked but Sal learned that the best thing to do was not to think about it but just get on with the job.

'Come on, Nar,' she called, perched at the top of the net. 'It's easy.'

'I don't know.' Narrinder placed her feet on the lowest ropes. 'It sways about a bit.'

'Nothing to it.' Sal flipped over the top and rapidly descended the far side of the net on her stomach. 'I'll give you a push,' she said, running around behind Narrinder.

'No, don't. I'll fall.'

'Don't be daft.' Sal climbed up next to her friend. 'Nothing to it. Watch.'

As she clambered higher the net swung from side to side like a curtain in a breeze. Narrinder clung on as she pitched to and fro.

'Sal, it's moving!'

'Course it is. You move as well. Sway with it.'

Narrinder followed her advice. Unfortunately her timing was out. The net swung upwards to her right, she leaned to the left and gracefully somersaulted over the edge of the ropes onto the soft wood chippings below.

'You all right?' Bill was there in seconds.

'Yes. I think so.' Narrinder brushed herself down.

'Need to move one hand and one foot at the same time.' Bill demonstrated and then looked at his watch. 'Time to start the course. Up the ladder into the tree

the swing, jump along the tyres, walk across
e,' he pointed to a thin piece of wood about a
e off the ground, 'then it's the net, crawl through
the rat tunnel, up the tree, across the rope bridge and
down the last rope swing. Got it?'

'Yes,' said Sal and the others. All except Tag.

'No,' he said quietly.

'Ah, remember you,' said Bill. 'This isn't as bad as
the death slide. The others can help you.'

'Can't do it, sir.' Tag hung his head in shame. His
fear of heights paralysed him.

'Well, have a go.'

Sal went first and quickly completed the course. The
only bad bit was the rat tunnel. It was a long canvas
tube half buried in the soil. Inside was dark and creepy
and it was easy to imagine that monsters, let alone rats,
lived there. She waited at the end of the course for the
next team member to appear. She waited and waited. At
last Cowboy turned up.

'Come on, you slowcoach,' she called.

'I am. It's Tag. He's stuck. The others are helping.'

Cowboy swung down to land next to Sal. 'And Narrinder doesn't like the rope bridge.'

At least she's got that far, thought Sal, going off to
encourage her.

'Get a move on, you wally!' she yelled at the still dark
figure swaying above her head. 'Just do it, or I'll never
talk to you again!'

'Good!' replied Narrinder, with unaccustomed spirit.
'Suits me!'

'Just shuffle your hands along the support ropes and
your feet will follow.' Sal prodded the bottom of her
friend's trainers with a stick.

'You're a bully, Sally Musgrove.' But Narrinder got
moving and soon joined them.

'Twenty minutes already,' said Sal grabbing Cowboy's
arm to look at his watch. 'Let's get the others.'

They rounded the tree and came into the clearing. What a sight! Vicki, as immaculate as ever, was sitting on top of the net, her hands outstretched to Tag. Brian was trying unsuccessfully to force Tag's reluctant feet into the right places. And Tag? He lay on his stomach on the net, like a stranded whale, eyes shut, knuckles showing white where his hands gripped the ropes tightly.

Vicki reached down and grabbed him by the shoulders of his jumper. At the same time Brian prised loose his reluctant fingers.

'Shove!' called Vicki, as Tag was heaved up like a sack of coal and dropped over the top of the net. He was too heavy for them to turn round, so he made his descent head first. Vicki and Brian hung on to him so that he would not shoot off the end of the net. At last a trembling Tag was on safe ground ready to face the terrors of the rat tunnel.

'Well done,' said Bill. 'Told you he could do it.'

'Him?' said Sal. 'It was *them* not *him*. They heaved him. He's useless.'

Bill looked at the muddy thin girl in front of him and sighed. 'Were you scared of the net?'

'Course not.'

'So it was no big deal to get over it?'

'No.'

'Well, for Tag it was a big deal, a very big deal. He had to overcome his fear. He was very brave.'

'Brave!' Sal was indignant. 'He's a stupid pudding. And how long have we been anyway?'

'Oh, I've stopped timing you. Reckon your team's last.'

Sal was furious. Just managing to bite her tongue, she stomped off to the rope bridge. Tag would make even more of a fool of himself on that. Even more of a fool of *her*. How could he be so pathetic, so dumb? If she had known he was going to be like this she would never have had him in the gang.

Now look at the great quivering lump of lard! Vicki in front, Brian behind, all on the rope bridge.

'Don't look down,' called Vicki. 'We'll help. Just pretend it's on the floor.'

'Where you'll be, when I get you,' said Sal, half under her breath.

It took over ten minutes to get Tag across the bridge and then he had the cheek to break into a smile.

'That was great,' said Brian.

'But what about the competition?' asked Sal.

'Stuff the competition. He did it. Isn't that great?'

'Sure.' Sal kicked the ground unconvinced. No-one said she was great when she sailed through the course and now this scaredy-cat was getting all the praise. She watched him dithering about, trying to get up the courage to descend the final rope swing. What a wally!

"As I have loved you." The words pierced Sal's brain with the accuracy of one of Bill's arrows. Well she was certainly not feeling love for Tag or anyone else at the moment. Just anger, like normal. What had Miss said? It was impossible without God's help.

Sal shot a prayer up through the leafy trees. 'Help. I'm at it again. Help me to love Tag.' She waited for the soft mushy feeling, like she had at the camp fire, to sweep over her. Nothing happened. 'And I'm sorry for being angry,' added Sal to her prayer. Still no wonderful glow to make her feel at peace with the whole world. Perhaps loving others was more than a feeling and giving them your hot-dog.

'Please show me what to do,' she prayed, at the same time walking towards where Tag should land off the rope swing. She smiled at him.

'Hey, Tag.' He did not look, expecting another mouthful off his hot-tempered team leader. 'You all right?' Tag was too amazed to reply. 'You've done really well. Come on, last little bit. Just hold on tight, shut your eyes and jump.'

Tag was so astonished that he followed her instructions and toppled in a tumbled heap at her feet.

'Are you feeling ill?' he asked.

'No, are you?'

Tag shrugged. Something weird had happened to Sal between the rope bridge and swing. Whatever it was it was a whole heap better than usual.

Bill rejoined them. 'I did time you. Fifty-eight minutes, nineteen point four seconds. I think you're last.'

'By much?' queried Narrinder.

'Well, the fourth team did it in, let's see, twenty-two minutes exactly.'

Tag glanced at Sal and waited for her to explode. Instead she started to laugh. The more she laughed the more the others joined in, until all six of them were shaking around.

'What's so funny?' asked Bill. This team were odd! But his question just made them double up all the more; the fear, tension and anger washed away by fits of giggles.

'Attention!' Bill clicked his heels together as the gang formed a shaky line. 'Well done, if a bit slow.' He glared at Sal which stopped her laughing again. 'We've just time for the abseiling before lunch.'

'Abseiling!'

'What's that?'

Bill ignored them and blew a sharp blast on his whistle. Like magic Lisa appeared, wearing a royal blue all-in-one suit. With her blond hair, she looked like an exotic bird picking its way through the trees. She and Bill led them deeper into the wood to the biggest tree they had ever seen. Planks were nailed up one side. On the other side there was a huge wooden wall that dropped sheer to the ground. It had no steps or handholds. Nothing.

Lisa sprinted up the planks like an Olympic runner

and disappeared.

'Send the first one, Bill.' No-one volunteered but at last Vicki was persuaded to go. At the top of the plank ladder there was a little platform, similar to the one on the death slide tree. Ropes were coiled on it and Lisa strapped Vicki into a harness that made her feel as if she were wearing a nappy.

'The idea,' shouted Bill so that they could all hear, 'is to go over the top of the wall and walk down it.'

'We'll be killed,' protested Sal.

'You hang onto the rope and come down backwards. The safety harness will hold you if you slip.'

Vicki made a safe descent. 'It's awful. Worse than the death slide. Terrible.' And she sat down to hide the fact that her legs were trembling.

At last Sal was at the top. Vicki was right. It was awful. To step off backwards into space holding onto a rope. She had seen soldiers doing it on telly but this was different. This was her doing it, for real. She wished the bell for dinner would rescue her but it stubbornly refused.

'Not scared, are you, Sal?' asked Lisa with a smile.

'No, course not,' said Sal, although all the colour had drained from her face and she was sure Lisa could hear her teeth chattering.

'Over the top then.' And Sal stepped out into nothing, feeling tremendous relief when the rope took her weight. Somehow she managed to slip and swung there on the safety harness, like a demented yoyo.

'Pull me up!' she yelled.

'Keep calm. Now just get your feet flat against the wall. That's right. Hold the rope tightly and down you go.' Sal's relief on reaching the ground was indescribable. She was shaking too much to unclasp the harness and stood there while Bill released her.

'Don't do it, Tag,' she said, collapsing next to him. 'It'll kill you off.'

Tag looked at her. Sal telling him not to have a go?

'It's a bit scary, just a bit, and I know you don't like heights.'

'Are you sure you feel okay?' Tag was puzzled.

'Yes, well, no, I mean I'm not sure.' Sal stumbled to a halt.

'So?' asked Tag.

'Tag, I'm sorry for being nasty to you, about you being a wally on the things. I got really mad.'

'I had noticed!'

'Well, I don't want to be.' Sal paused. 'Mad. I want to do more "as I have loved you".'

'You what?' Tag was lost and Sal felt a bit embarrassed.

'Love not anger.' Sal did not know how to explain and Tag was not that bothered.

'Fine by me,' he said, as the dinner bell broke through the silence and they trudged off.

The chips were ace. The weird shapes and chunks of peel added to their taste. There were loads of them. Sal sat by Tag. She still had not got a warm glow inside her but she knew that Jesus had helped her to replace the anger with love.

Love was strange. It wasn't just being kind or nice, it was more than that. It was sort of doing what was the best for someone else, even when you didn't want to. Like Tag. It was best to accept his fear of heights even if she could not understand them. And to let him know that it was okay to be afraid. No wonder Miss had said that there was nothing easy about loving others.

9

After lunch they were all herded into the games room. Bill gave them a lecture on the different trees and plants at Greenlands. It was so boring that Sal could have screamed. As far as she was concerned trees were big and you climbed them, while plants were small and for walking through.

The lecture improved greatly when Kevin and Lisa appeared. Kevin was cradling the fox cubs, one in each big gentle hand. Lisa had an owl perched on the thick sleeve of her jumper.

'Sometimes,' began Kevin, 'animals and birds get injured and need looking after. We've usually got something here at Greenlands. The cubs' mother was killed.'

'How?' interrupted Brian.

'The hunt.'

Sal was disgusted. 'But that's awful.'

'It's how things happen in the country,' said Kevin. 'Foxes have been hunted for centuries. They can be a pest.'

'But they're lovely,' protested Sal, reaching out to stroke them.

'Like this, yes. But when they've grown they can create havoc in a hen run.'

'What'll you do with them?' asked Brian.

'Release them when they are old enough,' said Kevin.

'But they might get killed, hunted,' Sal said.

'True. I know it's hard to understand but that's the way it is. Anyway, who wants to hold them?'

Sal was the first. As she stroked the cub, she had a

sudden pang of homesickness. There were no huntsmen in the grey terraced streets where she lived. She could kidnap the fox and take him home. He could live in her bedroom. Mum would never know. Perhaps he could eat their leftovers. In fact she could tell Mum it was a stray puppy. Mum was always too busy to notice what was going on. Sal could take it on walks with a collar and lead.

Her daydreams ended abruptly as two tiny razor sharp teeth sank into her wrist. Sal dropped the cub, amid much laughter from the others. He could take his chance in the wild, she thought.

After holding the owl who was recovering from a road accident, they all had to write up their diaries. Then they were free to escape into the great outdoors and do whatever they liked.

Brian and Tag went off to collect leaves and identify them. The rest of the gang left them to it. The donkey field held far more interesting possibilities.

'They're lovely,' said Vicki, crooning over the three grey donkeys. 'I'm going to stay here and stroke them. What about you?'

Sal eyed them suspiciously. Okay, so they were definitely a lot smaller than the horses, but they were still big. And their teeth! Long yellow fangs that would be just as happy munching Sal as the short grass.

'Me and Narrinder and Cowboy will play on the fence,' Sal informed Vicki. 'Got to see who can stay on the longest.'

The sturdy post and rails fence was quite easy to walk on, the top rail being smooth and wide. Some of the rest of the class joined in, all wobbling along, arms outstretched to balance. Tag watched from the edge of the wood, glad that he had gone leaf hunting.

'Play chase!' Sal said. 'I'm on. If you fall off, you're out, or if I catch you.'

The fence shook wildly as the children's feet pounded

along it. At regular intervals they fell off, Sal included, but they bounced up again unharmed. All this time the donkeys carried on eating, more bothered by Vicki stroking them than the wild antics on the fence. They had lived in the field for a long time and evidence of this lay everywhere in the form of dried dung.

No-one was ever sure who started it but people wobbling on fences make great targets for dried donkey dung. Grey pellets shot everywhere, breaking up into smaller pieces. The stuff was hard on the outside but crumbled on impact. It had been there so long that it did not smell too bad.

'Got you!' Sal dropped a clump down Tom's neck. He got her back by jumping on her and rolling her in it. Little bits of dung stuck all over her hairy jumper.

Still the placid donkeys munched on, while droppings whizzed past them.

'Eh, Sal,' Vicki called. 'What's up with Narrinder?'

Narrinder was sitting on the grass on the other side of the fence. Her head was bent low. Usually her long hair was held back in two tight plaits. Her mum did them every morning. On camp there was no Mum to do them and Narrinder's own efforts were feeble. All her thick glossy hair had escaped and tangled in amongst it were donkey droppings.

She was nearly in tears. 'It's all your fault,' she said to Sal.

Sal was immediately on the defensive. 'Ain't, I didn't start it.' She was just about to walk angrily away so she could leave the cry baby alone, when she stopped. Narrinder was really upset. This was a big deal to her, like heights were to Tag.

I'll never understand her, or anybody, thought Sal, who was completely unbothered by the muck dangling in her own hair.

'Come on, I'll help.' Sal sat down by her friend. Slowly and gently she picked out all the bits of dung. There were lots, like fish caught in a net, and just as difficult to get out. Sal was so intent on her task that she did not realise that she was missing out on the dung-fence game that was still in progress.

'I hate it. It makes me feel sick.' Narrinder looked as if she meant it.

'Don't fuss, I've nearly finished. Look, if it helps you, I'll go with you to find Brian and Tag. You can collect leaves with them.'

'And with you?'

Sal smiled. Helping Narrinder was one thing but collecting leaves was taking the friendship too far. 'Not likely. I want to be here for round two.'

As they searched the edge of the wood, Sal was thoughtful. She was also amazed. At herself. Usually she would have got mad at Narrinder for being such a fusspot, but she had not. In fact she had helped her and missed out on the game. She grinned to herself. If she had not been there herself, she would not have believed it. Perhaps this loving others would get easier the more she did it.

After depositing Narrinder with Brian, Sal spent the rest of the afternoon around the donkey field. Miss Winter found her and about eight others there. She sent them off to the showers and they finally emerged clean, sweet smelling and starving for tea.

Tea was late and afterwards it was starting to get dark. Bill appeared, wearing a camouflage jacket as well as trousers.

'Not another lecture,' groaned Sal, as Bill talked on and on.

'I found beech and oak and sycamore and pine . . .' said Brian.

'Big deal.'

'And there's one torch per group,' said Bill.

'What for?' Sal whispered.

'Orienteering.' Vicki had been listening. She particularly wanted to be friendly with Sal tonight because it was the last chance. Be better to wait until after the night hike to get her to agree. 'Bill gives us this map and we have to read it and follow the white blazes.'

'White blazes?'

'Marks on the trees. And collect stickers. You'll see.' Vicki informed her.

Sal's team were third to go.

'Now remember,' said Bill, 'you must take a sticker from each of the trees with white paint on them. Stick them down the edge of your map. And here's your compass.'

By silent agreement the compass was given to Brian the brain. He seemed to have been listening when Bill had gone on about how to use it.

'Right, start now,' Bill clicked his big stop-watch. 'And remember to clock in when you've finished.'

Sal had not realised how big the woods were. In the daytime they seemed light and airy. In fact she had been too busy to notice them. Now it was different. Huge pillars of trunks reared up in front of her and above her head leaves whispered and chattered to each other in the evening breeze. Long thin branches reached out to tease her and tap her on the shoulder, while the scrubby undergrowth tugged at her legs.

'Here, give me the torch,' Sal called.

'I need it,' Brian was insistent, 'unless you want to read the map.'

'No, I'll help you. Let's have a look.' The arrowed route zig-zagged between numbers before returning to the start. 'What's these?' Sal asked, pointing to the numbers.

'The trees. One to sixteen. We're supposed to find them in order,' and Brian continued to lead the way, the flickering light scarcely making any impression in the deep darkness.

'Here's one,' called Vicki. 'Number eleven.'

'Supposed to find number one first,' said Brian.

'Well, where is it?' asked Vicki.

'Dunno.'

'Look, put the sticker here and we'll fit the others round it when we find them.' Vicki organised them. 'Come on, we'll be here forever. Let's run.'

Off they jogged, accidentally stumbling across white blazed trees, collecting numbers in any old order.

'Straight on, then swerve left,' said Brian, fiddling with the compass.

'Have you any idea what you're doing?' asked Vicki.

'Course, follow me,' and Brian led them deeper into the wood, unaware that his map was upside down. He had not noticed the little arrow pointing north on the map and so had just guessed which way to go. As he was always right the others followed blindly.

They went deeper and deeper into the wood, the canopy of leaves blocking out the struggling moonlight. Through thick leaf mould that clung to their shoes, over fallen logs which smelt like rotting apples, on and on they tramped.

'We haven't found one for ages,' said Sal.

'Stop fussing. Nine and seven should be down here, by the lake.' Brian's faith in his map reading abilities held strong.

'What lake? I can't see it,' Sal said.

'Well, you will soon. Look, there's a bit of a clearing. Let's run.'

They set off, squealing and laughing. All except Sal. Something had reached up a monstrous slimy hand and caught her round her ankle. Over she went into a pile of dry ferns that scratched at her unprotected face. She lay there, winded, waiting for her breath to return to her body. At last she could feel her lungs going back to normal.

'Hey, wait!' she yelled. But no-one answered. Far away she could hear muted crashings through the undergrowth. 'Brian! Wait!'

Sal sat up and worked her foot loose from the gnarled tree root that had tripped her up. She listened. Nothing. Just the leaves talking to each other and a dry rasping sound, which she realised was her own breath.

'Help! Please help!' she called and then carried on talking to herself. 'This is awful. I can't see. I don't know where I am. I'm lost.' A scurrying sound made her jump. 'And I'll be got by the wild animals.' What if there were a fox nearby, out hunting, his teeth bared ready to sink into whatever he found? Or maybe owls cruised silently through the wood. One could hit her face. She screamed at the thought. And bats! Didn't they come out at night?

Sal got up and set off, just walking, not knowing where. Nights in the forest were the stuff that fairy tales were made of. She imagined imps and goblins round every corner, witches and werewolves leading her astray. Her eyes could make out the shapes of the trees and the huge ancient trunks took on evil personalities. Ogres and giants laughed at her feeble attempts to escape them.

Her heart was at it again, bump thumping away. She could not even see her feet but somehow they must be obeying her brain because they kept on walking. Brambles caught at her, their barbs embedding themselves in her clothes and scratching her face.

Fear rose up inside her. Sal felt sick. She would be lost in this wood forever. She would keep walking until she dropped down in exhaustion. They would find her months later, a mere skeleton. Perhaps they could identify her from her clothes. And Mum would never forgive her if she didn't return from Greenlands.

A pale streak danced into her vision. It looked like a smile, without a head, and Sal clasped her fists tightly as she went to investigate. Tree number eight. Safety! She collapsed into a heap, her back leaning on the best tree in the world.

Slowly her brain reactivated itself. Her team were third to do orienteering. That meant two more after them. Well, she had probably missed the fourth team, but maybe the last would be here soon.

Sal sat and waited, crunched up as small as she could. Her heart seemed to have gone back to the right place and she felt cold. In the distance a light flickered.

'Here!' She jumped up. 'Number eight! I'm at number eight.'

Peter Wilkins looked at her. 'What are you doing?'

'I fell. The others left me, so I decided to wait by a tree.' Sal conveniently left out the bit about wandering panic-stricken through the wood. 'I'll follow you lot.'

Making sure she was in the middle of the group, Sal trudged on. She felt weak and wobbly, relief flooding over her, turning her legs to jelly. If she wasn't careful she would cry and that would be awful. However, she could not prevent a few tears blobbing down her scratched face. Thank goodness it was too dark for the others to see her.

'Nearly done, one more,' called Peter, a few minutes later. Sal was astonished. Her team had walked miles, obviously the wrong way. She was quiet and thoughtful as they walked towards the welcome lights of civilisation.

She had been scared, really terrified. It was awful. That's what it must have been like for Tag on the net and rope bridge. He must have been afraid, just the same as she was. Perhaps it was okay to be frightened. I mean, she thought, I couldn't stop being scared. I just was. And Tag. He couldn't stop it either. I was scared of the dark wood and he's scared of heights. In fact, she realised suddenly, we're both the same. We're both yellow-bellied scaredy cats. Mind you, I won't tell him that!

Gratefully Sal met up with the others.

'We got to the road and walked back up it,' explained Brian. 'That's when we saw you weren't there. But we knew you'd be okay.'

'I was.' Sal gave him an unconvincing grin.

'Anyway, we're last again,' said Brian.

'What a surprise!' and Sal burst into gulping laughter as the fear and relief of the last half hour combined. 'Wouldn't want to spoil our record, would we? The last team at everything.'

10

Sal decided that she would be glad when it was bedtime. Her scratches stung her face and she felt worn out by the day's activities. She was folded into one of the saggy armchairs watching Mr Rogers beating everyone at table-tennis when Vicki came up to her.

'You've got to help me,' said Vicki.

'What?'

'You promised. When I helped you get Kevin's hat.'

Sal vaguely remembered. 'What?' she said again.

'I'll tell you outside, but you've got to do it.'

'Tell me here. I'm tired.' Whatever it was, it couldn't be that exciting. Vicki wasn't known for her brilliant ideas. She pushed Sal upright and marched her out of the room.

'Now, while everyone is lazing around. It won't take long.' Sal had never seen Vicki so determined. 'Right, follow me. Do you want your anorak?'

'I'm not going back in that wood.'

'No-one said that, silly.' Vicki threw her anorak to her. 'I put them here in case.'

'In case what?'

'You'll see.' Vicki walked briskly down the rutted lane. She had done this route many times and the darkness did not bother her.

'Not the horses! Why didn't you just say you wanted to see the horses? What's the big fuss?'

'I don't just want to see them.'

'Feed them, then. You've been doing that all camp.' Really, Vicki was nuts, thought Sal. Feeding them in the daytime when she could see them was bad enough. But at night? They'd never tell fingers from grass, even if they were awake.

'Ride them,' said Vicki.

'You can't. It's not allowed. Anyway, why do you need me?'

'Cos you're going to ride Silver,' she pointed to a huge muscle rippling white shape, 'and I'll have Dusty. That's what I've called them.'

'But I can't ride, and we mustn't, and where's the saddle things?' Sal was rapidly moving away.

'Sally Musgrove, you owe me this one, you've got to.'

'But Bill said we mustn't, not even go near them.' Sal remembered her new found intention to do what she was told. She had told Jesus she would keep out of trouble and horse riding was going to be one big trouble.

'When have you ever bothered about doing what you are told? You organised the midnight feast, and the daft games the night before. You got us all to join in. All I want is for you to join in *my* idea.'

Sal was stuck for words. How could she explain to this horse mad wally that she was trying to follow Jesus by doing what was right? Vicki would never understand.

'We can't and that's that.'

'You're scared!' Vicki touched a raw nerve. 'It's nothing to do with what Bill said. You're scared. Admit it! Sally Musgrove a yellow-belly. Wait until I tell Tag and the others.'

Sal tried once more. 'I'm not, it isn't that. We're not supposed to do it.' No way was she telling Vicki that the horses frightened the life out of her.

'Scaredy-scaredy Sally, like a little baby!' Vicki jeered at her.

'I'll watch you.' Sal compromised.

'No, both of us.' Vicki called Silver and Dusty over to the fence.

'But we need things to hold on to,' said Sal.

'Bridles? No, we'll be all right. Just hang on to the mane. Climb onto the fence and swing your leg over his back. Look.'

Vicki got on Dusty who did not seem in the least bit bothered.

'Come on, please. You promised.'

Sal leant on the fence. She was in a no-win situation. Vicki was right. She *had* promised. But she had also promised Jesus that she would do what was right. One or other of them would be let down.

'Look, it's easy. Just sit there, then we'll walk across the field. That's all. Honestly.' Vicki tried to persuade her.

Undecided Sal stayed where she was. Perhaps the horse would not seem so big once she was on him. Into her mind there flashed a picture of Miss Winter's face looking sad. That's how Jesus would look at her if he was here. But he wasn't. If he was, he could explain it all to Vicki and she would understand.

'Come on, hurry up, or the others will notice we've gone.' Vicki would keep up this badgering all night if she needed to. Sal climbed the fence and Silver nuzzled up to her. She would pretend that it was not happening. And anyway it could not be any worse than bouncing around on Kevin's shoulders. And Vicki was right. No-one would ever know. From now on, vowed Sal, I'm not promising anybody anything, ever!

Silver eventually lined up by the fence.

'Now Sal, go for it!'

Sal went for it. Grabbing a huge tuft of coarse stringy mane, she shut her eyes as she leapt onto the horse's back. His coat was slippery and a ridge of backbone stuck into her bottom. She wriggled about, certain that she would fall off any second.

'Relax, grip him with your inside leg muscles. Sit up straight.'

Relax! thought Sal. Vicki was mad. The moon reappeared from behind a thick cloud and bathed the field in ghostly light. It reflected off Silver's thick coat and turned the grass into a higgledy piggledy patchwork of dark and light.

'Great,' said Vicki. 'We can see where we are going.'

'I'm not going anywhere.'

Vicki ignored her. 'I expect Silver will follow Dusty. Walk on, boy,' and Dusty ambled off under Vicki's expert guidance.

Sal followed. She had no option. It was stay on or fall off. She clung to the mane as if her life depended on it, her body jolting completely out of rhythm with the horse's step.

'Look up!' Vicki called out instructions. 'Isn't this marvellous. The best bit of camp!'

'Marvellous!' echoed Sal, meaning the opposite. A huge head turned round and a thick pink rubber-like tongue licked her leg where her thin trousers had rolled up. It felt revolting. 'Let's get off now,' said Sal. 'You said across the field and back.'

Vicki knew when she was defeated. 'Okay.' Turning Dusty, she trotted gracefully across the grass, leaving Sal to bump painfully behind on Silver.

In a nearby road a car backfired, the sound carrying like a rifle shot through the silent night air.

Dusty and Silver neighed, reeled round and galloped back down the field. Sal survived the whinny noise but nothing else. As Silver turned she kept straight on, arched through the air and landed with a thud on the grass. Something hit her across the leg.

For the second time that night Sal lay in the dark, outside in a hostile world. She was breathing okay but kept still. Her leg was killing her and she dare not move it. Even the fear that Silver might return and trample her to death failed to shift her.

'Vicki!' she called, trying to make as little noise as possible. 'Vicki, where are you? I'm dying!'

She heard the thud of Vicki's boots before she saw her. Vicki bent over her friend, blocking out the fitful moonlight.

'You all right?'

'No. I can't move.'

'Course you can.' Vicki did not know how to cope with a stationary Sal lying in the middle of a field, especially when it would soon be time for lights out.

A huge silver head appeared, snuffling like a runny-nosed toddler, and Sal sat up quickly.

'He won't hurt you,' Vicki said. 'He's ever so gentle.'

'He already has. Look at my leg.'

'I can't see anything. It's too dark.' Vicki felt along Sal's body until a screech of agony showed her that she had reached the right spot. Vicki pulled her hand away, aware that it felt warm and sticky.

'I think you've been kicked, just a bit.'

'A bit! I'll never walk again. Just get me out of here.'

Fortunately Vicki was a lot taller and broader than Sal. She hooked her hands under Sal's armpits and dragged and pulled her across the field.

Sal would never forget the nightmare journey. Her leg was on fire, her skinny bottom bumped through the tufted grass, her arms pulled out of their sockets by Vicki's efforts. And all the while the two horses circled, curious to see what was happening.

Exhausted, Sal rolled under the fence and lay there. Vicki collapsed next to her.

'I told you not to do it,' said Sal.

'Well, how was I to know you'd fall off?'

'It wasn't the fall. It was the kick. Now, what are we going to do?'

'Don't know. Let's think.'

Sal was angry now. Here she was, in a right mess, writhing in agony, bleeding to death, in need of urgent help and all she'd got was brainless Vicki.

'I can't drag you up to the dorms,' said Vicki. 'I don't

know what to do. Can't you walk?'

'Walk? I'll probably have to have it cut off. For goodness sake get some help.'

'Miss Winter? Or Mr Wilkins?'

'Not one of them, you pea brain, or they'll know about the ride. Get the gang and tell them to be quiet.'

Vicki disappeared. Sal was worried. What if someone found out? What if she lay here for hours? Someone was bound to notice that she was missing. Gingerly she touched the top of her right leg. Looked like she'd ruined these trousers and she'd only had them last month. The pain was horrendous. She wanted to shout, scream, yell, but she did none of these.

'Oh, God, please get me out of this mess. Help me to get to bed. Please let me walk again.'

Tag, Cowboy and Brian appeared.

'Narrinder has gone to make your bunk. You didn't do it this morning. It's lights out in twenty minutes so we've got to move quickly.' Brian the brain was back in action. 'We'll sort of fireman's lift you.'

'Sort of' described it very well. Sal draped her arms round Tag and Vicki who were the biggest. Cowboy supported her backside, while Brian held the injured leg.

'Got to keep it straight,' he said, thankful that no-one asked him why.

Like an overgrown spider they stumbled and side-stepped up to the courtyard. Avoiding the splashes of light from the windows, they wove their way across the wide open space. A door opened, catching them in a beam of light.

'Ah, you lot. Sal's team.' It was Miss Winter. 'I wondered where you were.' She started to move towards them.

'Run,' Sal hissed, and then called out. 'We're just having a game, Miss, going to bed in a minute.'

'I expect you're tired, Sal, what with your wanderings

in the wood.'

'Yes, Miss, goodnight, Miss.' Sal breathed a sigh of relief. The adventure in the wood was nothing compared to this.

The gang rolled her onto Narrinder's bottom bunk. Cowboy took guard at the door as boys were banned from the girls' dorm. Sal lay groaning and moaning.

'Er, it's awful,' said Narrinder. 'Look.'

'Gosh!'

'Wow!'

'Stop staring and do something,' said Sal.

'But it's all stuck. Your trousers, the blood's stuck them into the cut, or whatever. You've ripped them.'

'Narrinder, get them off,' begged Sal.

'It'll hurt!' Narrinder gently unzipped the trousers and rolled them down as far as the bloody patch. 'Here, bite this.' She passed Sal a pillow. 'I saw it in a film. This woman was having a baby and there were no pain-killers so they boiled hot water and . . .'

'Get a move on,' choked Sal through a mouthful of pillow. She twitched violently. It felt as if her skin was being torn off. The blood started to trickle again.

'I'll have to get Miss,' said Narrinder.

'No, don't.'

'But it's bleeding and you're going to have an enor-mous bruise.'

'It must have been the horseshoe, the nails. They caught her skin,' said Vicki. 'That's why it's such a mess.'

'Thanks a lot,' said Sal. 'Just clean it up.'

Vicki found one of her clean T-shirts and dampened it. Narrinder carefully patted at the dried and fresh blood patterning Sal's leg.

'You'll make a good nurse,' said Sal.

'Doctor, you mean.' Narrinder stopped the bleeding. 'Now this might hurt.' She grabbed Sal's leg and twisted it round before bending it at the knee. Sal yelped in pain.

'Just testing nothing is broken,' said Narrinder.

'When my cousin broke his wrist,' began Tag, 'the doctor bent it round to check.'

'Well, I think it's okay. You'll have to walk to make sure,' said Narrinder.

'Can't.'

'Well, if you don't I'll fetch Miss Winter,' threatened Narrinder.

Sal rolled off the bunk and just managed to hobble to the loo, leaning on Vicki. Collapsing back on Narrinder's bed, she assured them that she would be okay. They must not tell anyone, not even the rest of the class, or the staff would find out.

The boys returned to their dorm as the other children came to get ready for bed.

'What are we playing tonight?' called Marie. 'Hey, why have you two swopped bunks?'

'We wanted to. And we're not playing anything tonight,' called Narrinder. 'Go to sleep.' But sleep would not come for a long time for Sal. She could feel her leg oozing onto the borrowed circus tent dress. Her face tingled from the scratches in the wood. Even the dying bruise on her arm from archery was throbbing. Her leg felt as if it had been pounded raw by a hammer.

Thank goodness they were going home tomorrow afternoon. She had only got to survive until then. If only she could keep her damaged leg a secret for a few hours then no-one would find out how she had done it. If only, she thought, I'd done what I knew was right. Then I wouldn't be in this mess!

11

Sal woke up feeling like an Egyptian mummy entombed in one of the Pyramids. She was lying flat on her back, twisted in her sleeping bag and wondering what the huge black shape was above her. A stab of pain shot down her leg and quickly reminded her that she was trapped in the bottom bunk bed.

'Narrinder!' Sal poked the sleeping lump above her. 'Narrinder, wake up, you've got to help me get up.'

'Too early.'

'But my leg! You've got to help me sort it out, before anyone sees.'

Two elegant brown feet appeared, followed by long legs that slid like snakes onto the floor. Narrinder untangled Sal and half carried her to the bathroom.

'Well, it's not bleeding,' she said, pulling the borrowed dress off the wound. Immediately fresh blobs of blood appeared.

'Just bandage it, or something.'

'What with?'

Sal pointed to Narrinder's pyjamas. 'They'll do,' and despite protests, Narrinder was persuaded to wrap them round Sal's leg. They managed to pull a pair of Vicki's long bermuda shorts over the top. No matter how Sal stood, she could not disguise the fact that one leg was now three times wider than the other.

The gang were first into breakfast and made sure that Sal had everything she needed. Her injury had not affected her appetite.

Miss Winter approached them. 'Sal, your team and

Peter's are in the one-man kayaks this morning, so will you hurry up and get down to the lake.'

'In a minute, Miss. Tag's just having some more toast.' Sal elbowed him. 'Aren't you, Tag?'

'What? Er, yes, Miss.'

'No time for that, come on, I'll walk down to the lake with you. Kevin and Lisa will be waiting.' Miss Winter led the way out of the dining room.

Sal tried as hard as she could not to limp. It was useless. She could barely walk and her face was pale as the pain burnt through her.

'Come on, girls, don't dawdle.' Miss Winter glanced at the three of them. They seemed to be having some sort of three-legged race. She took another look. Something red, silky and shiny was escaping from one of the leg's of Sal's bermuda shorts. What was she up to now? Miss Winter decided to ignore it. After all, it was the last day and no-one wanted any more hassles.

However by the time they had reached the lake, Miss Winter could ignore it no longer.

'Sal, what's the matter? You look awful.'

'Nothing, Miss.'

'And what's this dangling down your leg?'

'My pyjamas,' said Narrinder. Sal sent her a look that meant shut up. 'She's got them on.'

'On? Wrapped round her leg, more like. Now what is going on?' Miss Winter was getting impatient. She sent the rest of the gang over to Kevin and sat down on the remains of the grass. Sal thankfully collapsed next to her.

'I banged my leg, Miss, and it hurts a bit.' Sal made the understatement of the year. 'So we wrapped the pyjamas round it.'

'I'd better look.'

'No, it's okay.'

'What did you bang it on?'

'The . . . the fence,' Sal improvised. 'Down by the

horses.'

Miss Winter looked puzzled. 'I don't often see the top of someone's leg hurt by a fence.'

'I was climbing, Miss.' Well, it was nearly true. She had had to climb on the fence to mount Silver.

Just then a thin trickle of blood seeped out of the shorts.

'Come on, Sal, let's go and clean it up.'

'But Miss, the kayaks!'

'When it's cleaned up. You know, Sally, there are times I don't understand you. When you got this,' she pointed to the fading archery bruise, 'you were quite proud of it and everyone knew about it. Then you told us all about your aches after the assault course. But now, you've obviously had a nasty bang and don't want to make a fuss. I just don't understand.'

But a few minutes later Miss Winter did understand. The top of Sal's leg was swollen. An angry bruise in purple and dark blue swept across her skin. In a couple of places the skin was broken and blood still oozed from the gashes. It would have looked like a fence post bruise except for one thing. The shape. The horseshoe shape. Not a complete shoe but about two-thirds of it, the gashes where the horseshoe nails had torn Sal's skin.

'A fence?' asked Miss Winter, softly as she gently bathed the damaged skin.

Sal hung her head, gazing intently at her feet.

'Looks like a horseshoe.'

'It is, Miss.'

'And that's why you didn't want any help.' Miss Winter paused. 'Come on, Sal, let's have the whole story.'

And out it all came. The confusion about what to do, the promise to Vicki, riding the horses, the kick, the fear of being found out.

'All this, Sal, because you didn't do what was right.' Miss Winter sighed. 'I thought you'd got the idea. You knew going near the horses was out of bounds.'

'I know, Miss, but I promised. I had to keep my promise.'

Miss Winter was thoughtful as she put cream and a huge crepe bandage on the leg. 'I can see that. It was difficult but you did know what was right and what was wrong, didn't you?'

'Yes, Miss, and I asked Jesus, well, I sort of thought about him, to help me do right, but I suppose,' Sal sniffled, 'it was easier to do what Vicki wanted.'

'It often is,' said Miss Winter,' it's called being tempted. That's why we pray "lead us not into temptation" in the Lord's Prayer.'

'I've mucked it up again,' said Sal.

Miss Winter put her arm around her. 'And it probably won't be the last time! But I think you can learn to talk things through quickly with God before making decisions. I know I have to do that all the time.'

Sal looked at her. It was hard to imagine Miss Winter wanting to do something wrong.

'Anyway, no kayaks for you today . . .'

'Aw, Miss.'

'It's not a punishment. Your leg's just not up to it. I'll tell you what, you can take some photos. Wait here a bit while I get my camera and deal with Vicki.'

Sal sat in the deserted games room counting the beats as her leg throbbed. What an end to the camp. Now everyone would know what had happened. She was always getting into trouble and messing things up and this time she had not wanted to.

'I'm sorry, Jesus,' she said, 'I've done it again. Please help me not to be led into temptation.' She paused. 'And help me to know what temptation is. I'm sorry I've let you down.' She fell silent, feeling sad. She had let Jesus down. Perhaps he was cross at her or getting fed up with her. Perhaps he had had enough of a ten year old girl who found mischief even when she was not looking for it.

But what about Miss Winter? She hadn't even told her off, just been kind and talked to her. And she'd made a great job of the bandages. Perhaps Jesus was more like that. Or maybe it was the other way round. Miss Winter was a bit like Jesus. What was it? 'As I have loved you.' Miss Winter was showing her love and Jesus was too. She need not be scared of him.

Sal was humming the song about loving others when Miss Winter came back with Vicki in tow.

'Vicki's told me all about it. She says it was her idea and you tried to stop her.' Miss Winter looked at the pair of them. 'Anyway, I've decided no kayaks for Vicki either. This time as a punishment.' She looked at Sal. 'I think your leg's punishment enough for you. Is that fair?'

'Yes, Miss.'

'So you can hobble around and take photos. Just don't fall into anything and ruin my camera.' She showed them how to work the camera.

Sal and Vicki sat by the lake watching the kayaks. The two teams were trying to get their canoes into a long line next to each other. When they were ready, Kevin climbed out of his and leapt from one canoe to another until he reached the bank.

'See, it's easy,' he called. 'Now it's your turn.'

One by one the children tried to copy him. The kayak line wobbled, they lost paddles and of course nearly everyone fell in. Even Tag had a go, wobbling precariously in his own kayak before tripping over and landing head first in the lake. He was fine. Water held no terrors for him.

Sal recorded it on film.

'Wish we could do it,' said Vicki.

'Me too, mind you this leg would never bend enough.'

'She's not bad though, is she?'

'Who?' asked Sal.

93

'Miss Winter. I mean, she could have gone berserk.'

'Not her style.'

Vicki was thoughtful. 'No, it's not. You see her at that church youth club, don't you?'

'Mmm, and Mr Rogers.'

'Are they dead religious?'

Sal wasn't sure what that meant. 'I don't think so. They just love Jesus and want to follow God's ways.'

'Do you?'

Sal felt strange. This was the first time one of her friends had asked her directly what she thought. She didn't want Vicki to think she was dead religious, whatever that was. But she didn't know how to explain what she felt.

'Well, do you?' insisted Vicki.

'Yes, I do.'

'Why?'

'Well, it was last term with the Easter project and everything. I started to think about God and I wanted to be a Christian, so I decided to follow Jesus.'

'But you're still a wally.'

'I know.' Sal's reply seemed to satisfy Vicki.

'I might come to the youth group, if that's okay,' said Vicki.

'Course. Now let's take some pictures of the assault course.'

'There's no-one on it.'

'There will be.'

Painfully she dragged herself across the climbing net and insisted Vicki photograph her without the bandage showing. After taking ages she was photographed on the rope bridge, at the entrance to the rat tunnel, on the bottom rung of the abseiling tree and pretending to land after letting go of the rope swing.

'They'll all be of you,' protested Vicki.

'Good! Come on, let's find some others.' She took pictures of the dorms and after getting Miss to put in another film, photographed the fox cubs as well as taking a special one of the horses for Vicki. It took a long time to limp from one spot to another and Vicki left her sitting in the grass by the cubs while she went off to see what was happening on the river.

Sal sat alone, very tired, her leg aching, the pain killers just starting to take effect. She felt quite happy. Camp had been great. It seemed as if she had been here for weeks not days. All the adventures, all the fun, it was ace. And this afternoon they had got to go back home.

She tickled Foxy with a long piece of straw. Sal did not want to go home. She wanted to stay here forever. She could become an instructor, not for archery though, and spend every single day messing about in canoes. If she practised, she could become the fastest person in the world on the assault course. And I bet, she thought, that river goes to the sea. I could canoe to the seaside and across the ocean and all round the world.

Her thoughts were interrupted by a happy yell of 'Hi, Man!' It was Kevin on his way to restock the tuckshop.

'You're the leg girl, aren't you?' He looked at Sal more closely. 'And that same one that pinched my hat.' Kevin was wearing a new creation in pink and purple stripes. 'It's nearly dinner time.'

He pulled the hand cart out of the shed. 'Need this to load all of your junk on. Better put the biggest piece of junk on first.'

He picked Sal up, put her on the cart and they trundled back to the courtyard. 'You've about ten minutes to pack.'

Vicki took pity on Sal and did her packing. It was not hard. Nearly everything was slightly damp and hanging in the drying room. Vicki stuffed it all in a black bin liner and finished neatly folding her own clothes.

Mrs Rowbottom was getting very harassed trying to return all the night-clothes she had washed to their rightful owners. Sal never saw hers again.

Eventually everything was piled outside. All the damp trainers were tied in pairs and heaped up like a smelly compost heap.

'We'll sort it out at school,' said Mrs Rowbottom. 'Perhaps their parents will know whose is what. They don't.'

The last meal. The last entry in the diary. The final goodbyes to Bill, Kevin and Lisa. The last hunt for things left behind in dorms. The last visit to the tuck shop to get enough food to keep them going on the two hour journey home.

No-one rushed to get on the coach. No-one tried to hurry Mr Wilkins up as he loaded luggage. No-one wanted to go home. Well, no-one aged about ten.

Miss Winter sank into her seat next to David Rogers.

'You look exhausted,' he said.

'I am. Thank goodness we only run a trip to Greenlands once a year. Those instructors deserve medals.'

'Miss!' a voice called. 'Miss, are you listening?'

'Yes, Marie, what is it?'

'Can we come again, in the summer term?'

Miss Winter smiled. 'You must be joking,' she said quietly, so that only David could hear. 'No way! It's booked up by other schools,' she called out loudly.

Sal sat staring out of the window. She was on the front seat, her leg stretched across the aisle. She didn't know how she would work it, but she would stay at Greenlands again. Greenlands was brill.